Chicken Soup

for the

Indian Soul.

Teens Talk
Relationships

This book belongs
to: Sai karra.

Chicken Soup
for the
Indian Soul.

Teens Talk
Relationships

Jack Canfield
Mark Victor Hansen
Raksha Bharadia

westland

We would like to acknowledge the following publishers and individuals for permission to reprint the following material. (Note: the stories that were penned anonymously or that are public domain are not included in this listing.)

Comic Crush. Reprinted by permission of Madhuri Jagadeesh. © 2011 Madhuri Jagadeesh.

Fairy Tales. Reprinted by permission of Reeti Roy. © 2011 Reeti Roy.

Free. Reprinted by permission of Nidhi Pathak. © 2011 Nidhi Pathak

(continued on page 339)

westland ltd

Venkat Towers, 165, P H Road, Maduravoyal, Chennai 600 095
No. 38/10 (New No. 5), Raghava Nagar, New Timber Yard Layout, Bangalore 560 026
Survey No. A-9, II Floor, Moula Ali Industrial Area, Moula Ali, Hyderabad 500 040
23/181, Anand Nagar, Nehru Road, Santacruz East, Mumbai 400 055
4322/3, Ansari Road, Daryaganj, New Delhi 110 002

Copyright © 2011 Chicken Soup for the Soul Publishing LLC

10 9 8 7 6 5 4 3 2 1

ISBN: 978-93-80658-76-6

This edition is published under arrangement with Chicken Soup for the Soul Publishing LLC, its logos and marks are trademarks of Chicken Soup for the Soul Publishing LLC

This edition is for sale in India, Pakistan, Bangladesh, Nepal and Sri Lanka only

Cover photograph courtesy Corbis Images
Inside book formatting and typesetting by Ram Das Lal

Printed at Aegean Offset Printers, Greater Noida

Contents

4. IN TOUGH TIMES

5. ON FAMILY AND LOVE

6. ACTS OF KINDNESS

7. EYE-OPENERS

8. PAINFUL PARTINGS

9. SPREADING YOUR WINGS

10. MEMORABLE MOMENTS

11. IT'S NEVER TOO LATE

12. ON WISDOM

Introduction

We walked nervously into the assembly hall, whispering into each other's ears and giggling foolishly. Everybody had formed groups and had pledged to stick together. All the boys were gathered on one side, and the girls displayed a unified front by flocking to the other end of the hall. We were all ninth graders and it was our first prom night. Strains of the popular track by the Beatles, '*I saw her standing there ...*' resonated in the air but the dance floor was vacant. None of the 'cool dudes' could muster up the courage to be the trailblazer and ask a girl for a dance. For them, the fear of rejection was overwhelming and nobody wanted to risk a battering of the ego. The girls put up a pretence of lack of interest while silently sending up prayers to not end up as wall flowers for the evening. An array of varied emotions, an anxious step on the threshold of adolescence, king-sized ambitions and an eagerness to explore life....

Welcome to *Chicken Soup for the Indian Soul: Teens Talk Relationships*! Teens — those wonderful growing years are marked by a profusion of energy and excitement, but can be just as tough and trying. My contributing authors have shared poignant and hilarious incidents that highlight the innocence and confused perceptions associated with the time. The flutter of butterflies in the stomach as awareness of the opposite sex builds up and often controls the behaviour of teens makes for endearing stories. The bliss of falling in love, the somersaulting heart, the first crush and the following string of crushes, all come with its share of heartaches and heartbreaks. I have some touching anecdotes, narrated with passion and humour that describe the vulnerability and uncertainty one experiences at this age.

These stories give us an insight into the mindset of teenagers, and help us understand them as individuals trying to get a foothold for themselves in this big world. As we all eventually learn, life is not always on an upswing, it may just decide to take a u-turn and bring us crashing down. My contributing authors have shared several such incidents from their lives and how they succeeded in coming out of it stronger and wiser. Many of these pearls of wisdom are precious and worth preserving for the rest of our lives.

There is a Jewish adage that says 'who finds a faithful friend finds a treasure'. We are not always fortunate enough to simply stumble upon true friends. Most of the time it turns out to be exactly like a wise man had aptly observed: 'Friends are like melons … to find a good one, you have to try a hundred!' I have an extensive range of stories on this wonderful aspect of life: friendship. These stories promise to transport my readers to the thrilling days of school and college, as it is mostly during those days that the seeds of friendship are planted. Some relationships blossom into eternal bonds whereas some bloom into saplings and then wither away. Some endure tempestuous storms while others merely succumb. You will be enamoured by the stories about beautiful friendships that flourish from a simple rendezvous at a coffee shop; about how camping trips facilitate bonding; and realise how essential it is to hold on to a true friend with both hands.

So, dear readers, gear up, get set and plunge into this wonderful yet challenging world of teenage years. You will be able to relate to these experiences with surprising ease as the floodgate of memories open up and carry you with the flow. If you are a teenager, you are sure to get a substantial insight into the wonders and complexities of your age. Believe me when I say this book has it all. And if these stories motivate you to pen down your own memorable experiences, do so by all means, and send it in to us right away!

Raksha Bharadia

1

ON GROWING UP

You have to do your own growing no matter how tall your grandfather was.

–Abraham Lincoln

Comic Crush

The *Superman* and *Spiderman* movies had just released in Bangalore, a pensioner's paradise then. Just as we entered our teens, America began making its entry into our town. Our Archie comic fantasies seemed to be coming alive with juicy slices of cheesy heaven, soda pop and cool joints.

We lived in a locality called Benson Town and my friend Ramona and I were the only two girls always playing with the boys. Games like cricket, football, badminton and monkey-on-the-tree were our favourites.

It was under the shade of a beautiful tamarind tree that both of us discovered that we actually liked two boys in our play group. These boys were brothers and we named them Superman and Spiderman. As we were talking, we realised a girl, one of our group, was eavesdropping on us sharing our school girl secrets.

One sunny afternoon we were going to play badminton with the boys and I proudly put on a red half-sleeved T-shirt with a beautiful shiny sticker of Porky Pig, a cartoon character. The T-shirt was from America and hence considered cool. It was my pride and joy. So with my shining new racquet swinging and my prized American T-shirt I set out to play our usual game. The game was going beautifully; Ramona and I were beating Superman and Spiderman hollow.

It was the last game and just as I was about to beat my comic book hero, he suddenly began riling me, asking was that my photograph on the T-shirt and if I looked like that, how could he ever find me pretty? Obviously the evil eavesdropper had spilled the beans.

My heart sank below Porky's picture. With tears of rage running down my face I charged towards him and began pummeling him. To defend himself and to spite me he pulled at the shiny sticker and poor Porky Pig came apart. Porky hung in tatters like my pride and I ran home filled with shame and humiliation.

But I slowly realised that I had outgrown playing with those silly boys. Ramona and I began ignoring and avoiding them. Our tomboyishness gradually disappeared.

Your first crush, first love, first movie — they begin to set you thinking about what you really want out of life. My first crush made me realise that if a boy really liked me, he would make me feel good about myself. Also, that learning to like myself was very important — even more important than anybody else liking me.

Madhuri Jagadeesh

Fairy Tales

The first story that I can remember being read to me was *Little Red Riding Hood*. Little Reeti Roy, all of three, would sit on her father's knee, wide-eyed with wonder, listening.

'Go to sleep, my angel, I'll read the rest of the story out to you tomorrow, otherwise Wee Willie Winky will come and get you. He doesn't like children who are up past their bedtime, my father would say. I would shudder at the thought of horrid Wee Willie Winky and then fall asleep thinking of Red Riding Hood and her beautiful brown basket full of goodies, her polished black shoes, her oh-so-pretty dress, her light brown hair and rosy cheeks....

'Wake up, sleepyhead. Today, I'm going to tell you the story about a magic golden dragon.' 'Really? Where does it live, Baba?' 'Oh, it lives here, in Kolkata, but you can't see it. It is afraid of human beings, so it won't appear in front of you. But you know the Golden Dragon loves broccoli. If you don't finish yours, it'll eat it all up.' Gobble ... gobble ... gobble ..., and voila! There would be no broccoli left on my plate. Another time, Baba told me that fairies danced with the goblins in the moonlight, and that toadstools were actually meant for their tea parties. I felt deprived after listening to these tales — why couldn't I be as small as them?

So you see this was the clever ploy employed by Baba to make sure I did exactly what I was supposed to. He never yelled at me but merely spun yards and yards of magical tales ... tales that I was enthralled by.

I grew up in a huge house, one of the few remaining ancestral mansions in Kolkata. As a result, there were big palm trees that swayed to the breeze and big banyan trees, which according to Ma housed 'Brahmadaityas' (Brahmins who have died and become ghosts).

The house had been built by my great-grandfather and some parts of it were so dilapidated that you couldn't even imagine living there. There were cobwebs on the wall; lizards, bats, squirrels and even snakes roamed all over the place. But this is what made my growing-up years magical and full of mystery.

There was a hidden tunnel in my bathroom which led to a small room. From the moment I discovered it, I wanted to shut myself in it, away from the world. I would seek solace in that small room. During one such phase of seclusion, I wrote a poem:

Dream on, you silly child, it shall not last.

What stories have you been told

of far, far away? Dragons, unicorns, magic wands ...

What will happen when you know

that they don't exist? What do you do, when you realise

that your whole life has been

a finely woven web of lies? Simple lies that you were told

so that you would not cry.

You cried, nevertheless ...

You cried aloud when your peacock died ...
and also when the sun didn't shine when you wanted it to.
Was it worth it?
Was it worth telling you stories that would silence
you momentarily
but haunt you till the end of time?

In retrospect, this made me wonder ... had I become a cynic? Had the fact that my parents told me so many stories affected me so deeply that when harsh reality looked me in the eye, I couldn't deal with it? It took me a while to distinguish between fiction and reality. How could fairy tales be my reality?

And then, Baba told me something that I will never forget. 'My angel, it is what you *choose* to believe in, that makes all the difference. Have faith, belief and everything will become crystal clear.'

I'm eighteen now, struggling with the pressures of everyday life and learning new things with each passing day. But what I know for sure is that what you believe in makes you who you are. So, never stop believing. And never stop having faith in yourself. I know I never will.

Reeti Roy

Free

'He doesn't love you, I am sure. And we all know that he is interested in Rita.' I am not sure what hurt me more — the fact that he didn't like me or that he liked someone I did not get along with.

All of a sudden, everything seemed to come to a standstill. The loud music playing in the dormitory was no longer audible but I could hear something else ... it was a sound coming from within me. Yes, it was the crash of my shattering heart!

It all started a few days back, when I spoke to him for the first time. Before that he was just a regular boy in school for me and I had hardly noticed him. Our conversation had lasted all of fifteen minutes and I was on cloud nine. I suddenly grew shy with him. Every day I came to school hoping to meet him and talk to him. Romantic songs and movies made me think of him.

I was discreet about my admiration and ensured that no one got to know about it. But others were smarter than I had anticipated. My strange behaviour and sudden loss of interest in the usual girly gossip aroused their suspicions and soon my friends put two and two together. They started teasing me and I didn't mind it at all. Love was in the air and I was in seventh heaven.

But now, I felt hurt. My friend Saloni shook me out of my state of shock. I looked at her helplessly. She seemed to understand but could do nothing except say that he did not deserve me and I would get someone much better. 'It is not the end of the world,' she said firmly. I didn't believe her and knew that these were just words of consolation. It felt devastating as I cried like a baby.

I was sad, wept frequently and skipped my meals for the next two days.

I was sad, wept once or twice but ate dinner on the third and fourth day.

I was sad, did not weep and ate all my meals on the fifth day.

I felt better on the sixth and seventh day.

On the eighth day, I joined the girly gossip hour and laughed away all my blues.

A month later, I was completely out of it.

The following day, I bumped into him outside class. I looked at him — my heart did not skip a beat. He handed me a notebook and asked me to give it to Rita.

'Sure,' I said, and smiled.

Nidhi Pathak

Main Invited Hoon Kya?

Udhav, my teenage son, made a phone call to his friend and asked, 'Main invited hoon kya?' My wife and I laughed at his innocence. It was a joy to see that he was still far from the typical over-exposed teenagers.

It was an interesting turn of events, which had forced Udhav to make that innocent call. A boy called Sidhantha, who had been his classmate for the last couple of years, shared his birthday with him. Udhav had already planned his birthday party, but when he learnt that Sidhantha too was throwing a party on the same day, he requested us to change the date for his party to the previous evening. 'Our friends will get divided,' was his simple logic. We agreed.

During his party, I asked him to introduce me to Sidhantha, the boy for whom he had changed his plans.

'He has not yet come,' was his brief reply. Sidhantha had been unable to make it to Udhav's birthday.

The next morning, Udhav reminded us that he had to go to Sidhantha's party. We enquired about the time and venue, but he did not know.

'Aren't you invited?' we asked him.

'Yes, I am. In the school dining room, when I asked him about the party, he told me that I was also invited. So I am!' He replied in excitement.

'But did he tell you about the venue and time?' I was surprised.

'No, but I can confirm with him,' he said, rushing to the telephone. He called Sidhantha and turned on the speaker phone.

'Happy birthday, Sidhantha! Where are you celebrating your birthday and what time is your party?' He came straight to the point.

'Let me ask my father,' Sidhantha replied hesitantly. After a long silence, he gave the details. He did not ask Udhav to be there.

'How can you go, Udhav? He has still not invited you,' we tried to reason with him.

Udhav tried to convince us for a few minutes and then marched straight to the telephone and called Sidhantha again. 'Hello, Sidhantha, main invited hoon kya?' He asked naively. We were shocked.

On the other side, Sidhantha too seemed to be confused and handed the phone to his father. Udhav greeted his friend's father politely and asked, 'Uncle, main Sidhantha ke birthday mein invited hoon na? 'It was a loaded question that left no room for denial from the other end. He was invited.

Jumping with joy, Udhav came running to us. 'Didn't I tell you that I am invited?' We were amused.

Udhav's simplicity was like a breath of fresh air. This was such a beautiful age when friendship was yet to be tainted with selfishness. Ego was no threat, vested interests did not take control of the purity in a relationship and all that mattered was having fun.

It was difficult for us, but we convinced him not to go. Maybe we should have let him.

Veerendra Mishra

Maya's Little Girl

'My little girl's growing up!' Maya thought as she watched Ria sitting demurely, knees together in a tight skirt, exactly like her elder sister, Dia, who was like the sun and the stars to her. All of Dia's mannerisms, gestures, her accent and even the way she dressed would be observed and emulated by little Ria. When her older sister was away at college and wouldn't take her calls, she'd sulk, but turn into her sister's shadow the instant she stepped home.

When Maya started noticing Dia's grimaces and irritation at her little sister's constant presence, she tried explaining to the little one, 'Sweetheart, Dia is grown up now. She has her own friends and places to go. It's a bit embarrassing if you follow her everywhere.'

Earlier Dia would play with her, buy her favourite books and spoil her silly. The two sisters had been inseparable, but all that was before Dia turned eighteen. Now she seemed to be more preoccupied with herself. Maya would often discuss the situation with her husband, Madhav. He would just smile and remark, 'They'll grow out of it! One day, the shoe will be on the other foot!'

Besides, now there was also Rakesh who had entered Dia's life, much to Ria's annoyance. 'Why does that boy always come over ... he is so yuuuckk!' Ria's lip would hang down petulantly as she demanded an answer from anyone within earshot. Maya would silence her with a finger on her lip, and Dia would roll her eyes impatiently.

'Ma, Ria is turning into a pest! Please tell her to stop snooping around,' Dia screamed. 'Yesterday she even dropped my favourite perfume bottle.' Maya sighed as she replied, 'Dia, she adores you and wants to be exactly like you. She is at that difficult stage ... '

'Ma, don't take her side!' exploded Dia. 'I am keeping my door locked now onwards.'

And so she did. The first time Ria saw the door locked, she stood with a puzzled expression, but when she realised that it was to keep her out, she burst into tears and ran to her mother. Maya held her gently, letting the storm abate on its own. When Ria was finally exhausted with her crying, she said gently, 'Baby, you need to let go! Dia loves you but she just needs privacy, you will too when you are her age ... so just let her be!'

'But Rakesh is allowed to read her diary and spend time with her ... that's not fair! He is not even her brother!' Maya hid her smile at the innocent remark. 'But he is a good friend, a very good friend!'

A few years went by, and Ria was now a bubbly young sixteen-year-old with loads of friends, most of them boys. She hardly seemed bothered about Rakesh anymore — though there were times when she would make a face on seeing him!

Dia never showed it, but it was quite apparent that she often missed her sister's clinginess. Then one day, Dia came home to find Ria's bedroom locked. She stared at the door, as confused as her sister had once been. She hurried to the drawing room where her parents sat, watching television. 'Ma, Dad, Ria has locked her bedroom door ... why!' She stopped short, as her parents burst out laughing! And then it struck her like a thunderbolt! The shoe was finally on the other foot!

Deepti Menon

My First Shave

Even Picasso experimented with it. He was a man, wasn't he? It doesn't elevate me to the level of Picasso, but it is true that I have also experimented with shaving like every other boy. I started as early as last century … in 1990, when I was still a young lad of fifteen.

I still cannot forget Gitanjali Iyer (of Doordarshan fame), who used to be my fantasy girl. Back then we did not have all these music albums with curvaceous babes on the television. Neither did we have Fashion TV.

I wanted to start shaving very early, but perhaps my father did not want me to grow up too soon for he asked me not to shave till I was at least eighteen. Being a fifteen-year-old boy in love with three girls at the same time — Gitanjali Iyer, Renuka Shahane and that neighbour aunty of mine — I did not listen to my father.

I smuggled my father's shaving kit to the bathroom. It wasn't the kind of bathroom you would like to shave in, especially if it was your first time. The mirror was decorated with soap marks and bindis left stranded by my sisters. The floor was slippery and I had to hold on to the door handle because the bolt inside was very feeble. The bucket would

always be full of clothes, the mug's handle was broken …
because it was as old as my parent's marriage!

Coming back to the shaving, back then, it was simple.
There was no Gillette Mach 3 and all you needed was a razor
with a Topaz blade and some shaving cream. The middle-
class used the green soap that came in a red, circular case.

I stood in my slippery bathroom staring at the young
lad in the mirror. I wanted to shave, and nothing was
going to stop me.

While I had decided to shave, I had also decided to keep it
a secret. I knew if my father found out that I had not listened
to him, he would order: 'Down … now give me thirty!'

Anyway, I could not keep it a secret because just when the
blade touched my virgin cheeks, I slipped and in the process
gave myself a very deep cut. The result: a loud scream
followed by my father pushing the bathroom door open
(remember, the bolt was loose). I was standing there, caught
with a razor in hand … and blood flowing down my cheek.

This antic of mine was different from the others. On
some other occasions, my father has caught me red-
handed but this time, he caught me red-faced. But after
this incident, I learnt that it is wiser to obey your father,
especially if he is an army man!

Jamshed Velayuda Rajan

The Ouija Ordeal

'Is this the right thing to do?' I asked Tania, my face quite pale with nervousness and fear, although I hated to admit it then. It was her thirteenth birthday, I was at her place for a sleepover. Sara was there, but she being older, wasn't that scared. In fact it was she who had gifted Tania the Ouija board. Tania's eyes were brimming with excitement; she was finally going to talk to her twin, Sonia. I wondered why Sara couldn't have given her a T-shirt like I did, I thought looking at my present, lying ignored under many other birthday gifts. For a moment, I hated Sara; not only had she given Tania her best birthday present, but also something so eerie.

'Aren't I always right?' Tania replied. I had always trusted her but this time it just didn't feel right.

'Are you scared?' asked Sara. I bit my lip not wanting to admit the obvious.

Sonia was Tania's photocopy, except for the colour of her eyes. She had green eyes. We were seven when she was diagnosed with jaundice. It was a time when everyone was getting jaundice, even I did, but her case was different, Mum had said. I had waved at her from the verandah the day she was going to the hospital. Her green eyes looked bright and scary against her pale yellow skin. She never returned. For an entire month after that, I felt as if she was following me.

Then one day, Papa got me a fur ball that made me forget all about ghosts and spirits. It was a small little puppy and being my un-imaginative self, I ended up calling it 'Doggy'. Eventually Mum started telling me that spirits didn't exist but in spite of being thirteen, I didn't believe her.

I used to get a feeling that someone was watching me whenever I was alone. I was sure it was Sonia. However, that feeling went away the moment Doggy came to me. But the thought of having her around, especially when Doggy was not there, was driving me nuts. I couldn't say it out loud either, for I had just turned thirteen three months back. No self-respecting teenager was allowed to feel or at least acknowledge publicly that she was scared.

'Scared? I have been a teenager for about three months now! 'I was just wondering if it is right to disturb spirits. Grown-ups don't,' I replied.

'Grown-ups do a lot of things we don't know,' Sara intervened, 'and I think this should be one of our secrets!'

Tania's eyes were gleaming; all our words were so inconsequential; she would talk to Sonia tonight. It was only at that moment I realised, after these six long years, how much she still missed her twin.

'I'm still not convinced about this! Why don't you do it tomorrow when I'm not there?' I asked.

'Because today when the clock strikes twelve, it is going to be Friday the thirteenth and it is a no moon night!'

'I don't believe in coincidences, but maybe Sonia wants to talk to me,' Tania said, not even looking straight at me;

she was busy getting the things ready. It would be twelve in about an hour.

'Yes, I don't believe in coincidences either,' continued Sara, 'I had just gone to buy her a checker board, when the old man there mentioned he had something special. It was an antique piece, he said, and took a newspaper-wrapped package out of a bag kept in the corner. It looked so mysterious I knew it was not meant for kids, but then I thought, you are turning thirteen. Moreover, I got a feeling as if I was being forced to take it. I don't know why though. It must have been Sonia working on me.'

They were spooking me out, by talking of Sonia like that. I wanted to go home, hug Doggy and go to sleep. But Tania wouldn't let me go. 'You must stay here! You knew Sonia.' Tania looked straight into my eyes, when she said this. She was desperate. Her eyes betrayed her feelings, though her voice didn't. Beyond all logic, her eyes revealed fear too. Although I wanted to run away, I couldn't leave her alone. After Sonia, I had been like a sister to her. At that point of time, I wanted to support her.

With thirty minutes left to twelve, everything was almost ready. Thirteen candles, a picture of Sonia, and some incense sticks were placed on the window sill. 'They will attract Sonia here,' Sara said.

A bottle of cold water and a metal cross had been kept, to drive away Sonia, in case she didn't want to go. The Ouija board had been placed in front of the window. We three sat in silence, waiting for midnight to strike. Suddenly Sara asked us a question: 'So what was it like, having her around?'

'Sonia was the timid one. Tania always protected her from everybody,' I said smiling at Tania. 'Even from their Mum sometimes. She first finished her homework and then quickly did Sonia's.' Tania smiled at this memory.

'I used to wake up five minutes early to pack her bag; she hated waking up … remember how you used to envy me for having a twin?' Tania asked. I nodded, overcome with emotion. I could neither speak nor could I stop the tears from escaping my eyes. Tears and nostalgia are infectious; Tania too started crying. We hugged each other and cried for what seemed like ages.

Sara, who had come to our neighbourhood only two years back, couldn't understand all this and suddenly broke our reverie, saying, 'Umm … stop crying both of you. You can speak to her now! It is time to wake up the sleeping spirit that has been resting for six years!'

Breaking away from my embrace, Tania enquired, 'Wake her up? Is she sleeping now?' Sara looked bemused and said, 'Don't you know what happens to people when they die? They go into an eternal sleep. That's why they write RIP on tombstones, it's "Rest in Peace".'

'But Sonia never liked being woken up,' Tania said.

'Doesn't matter, she is a spirit now. Spirits are different! I've always wanted to find out …' Sara continued.

But Tania interrupted, and holding my hand, she said, 'She may be a spirit to you but she is more than a spirit to us. I can't wake her up …'

It was at that moment that all my fears vanished and Sonia became more like an angel I knew rather than a ghost or spirit I feared. Through this Ouija ordeal, I had learnt another lesson of growing up. I wept: for Tania, for not trusting her, our memories, our childhood, our friendship. And in those tears, Sonia seemed more real than that Ouija board would have ever made her.

Joie Bose Chatterjee

2

ON LOVE

*Y*ou have to walk carefully in the beginning
of love; the running across fields into your
lover's arms can only come later when you're
sure they won't laugh if you trip.

                                    –Jonathan Carroll

A Love Nearly Missed

The girl who came to my clinic one evening seemed troubled. Her sober outfit in a pastel shade of blue reflected the sadness in her eyes. She didn't speak for a while and fidgeted with the end of her dupatta. She was probably in her early twenties. 'How can I help you?' I asked.

'I'm in love with my old school mate and we mean to get married,' her voice faltered as she went on, 'but now I'm not so sure it will work. I have so many doubts....'

'Premarital jitters?'

'Not exactly. I have a problem and I need to sort it out. Things were going smoothly for us until Sandeep confessed to me something he had done a long time ago. It has shaken me so much and I just can't seem to forgive him. Externally everything seems fine between us, and I'm sure he has no clue about this feeling simmering inside me. Can a person love somebody and still harbour an unforgiving spirit? I wonder if you can help me.'

Nandita then related the incident her fiancé had told her about. It had taken place years ago. It was the last day to pay the examination fees for her PUC exams ....

'I left it so late because my mother couldn't come up with

the amount required. You see, we were not well off, in fact we were struggling to make both ends meet. I had lost my father several years earlier, and we had difficulty managing on my mother's salary. She was a shop assistant in a sari shop. In the end, she had to pawn her gold ring to give me the money. But even before I could pay the amount, it had disappeared from my handbag. The deadline was 2 p.m. that day, and I just couldn't make any other arrangements. So I couldn't sit for the exams and lost one precious year.'

Sandeep had befriended her that year. Tears welled up in her eyes as she talked of her disappointment and her mother's anger over her carelessness. Sandeep went out of his way to comfort her and they became close friends. They continued to remain friends even after they parted ways. 'I found a job as a clerk in a private firm and he went on to become an engineer. We kept in touch regularly, and often met for a cup of coffee whenever possible. He was very kind and considerate, and it was easy to fall in love with him. I was thrilled when he proposed to me in spite of the disparity in our social status, and I readily accepted.

'Now he has confessed that it was he who had stolen the money from my bag that day as he wanted to party with his friends, and his father had refused to give him an allowance. "I was selfish," he said, "and at that time I felt my need was greater than yours. I didn't want to lose face in front of my friends."

'He felt no remorse at all, even though he knew I would lose a whole year. But now he wants to set things right between us before we take the plunge, and has begged me to forgive him. I know he is truly sorry for what he has done, and I told him it doesn't matter anymore.'

'But deep down in your heart you can't forgive him?'

'How can I? Sandeep could have confessed to me a long time ago. Why did he wait until after we decided to marry? I can't bring myself to forgive him neither do I want to break up with him. On one hand I love him, but deep within, I am angry and mistrustful. I feel this may come between us sooner or later unless I truly forgive him. This is what is making me miserable.'

'Look at me Nandita,' I said. 'He must have known he was taking a risk when he confessed to you. I'm sure he wants to start life on a clean slate. He could have kept it a secret forever, but because he loves you so much he wants nothing to spoil your relationship. Do you really love him and want to marry him?'

She nodded.

'Then you must learn to forgive.'

'Yes Ma'am. That's why I have come for help. I don't want to marry him with resentment in my heart.' We had several sessions together over the next two months. She had to learn to let go and forget the feelings that brought so much pain. But first she had to confront her own unforgiving nature before she could forgive Sandeep. 'You cannot erase yesterday,' I said, 'You don't want to be imprisoned by the past. Set yourself free for tomorrow.'

The sessions proved to be cathartic. When Nandita was actually able to voice words of forgiveness, she found profound relief in her relationship. She became her old cheerful self again

Almost two years after they were married, I met them at a function. They looked blissfully happy.

'Thank you for helping me shed my resentment,' she said. 'I have learnt that forgiving is an inseparable part of loving.'

'Yes,' said Sandeep. 'And I'm a very lucky guy.'

Eva Bell

A Tryst With My Identity

There is no rush like the rush you get when the 'latest-crush-in-your-life' looks at you from across a crowded room and smiles. It is as if all those boring thoughts of books and exams and fights have been replaced with this heady, giggly, nitrogen-filled bubble where there's just you and him! And there you go, planning exactly how he'll ask you out … what you'll say … what you'll wear for the first date … aah your first kiss ... walking away into the sunset and living happily ever after….

And that's the beauty of being a teen … you actually believe with all your heart that this is the exact sequence of events that will happen. But then, life happens!!

I was one of the most popular girls in my class. At any given time, I would be surrounded by at least two guys. Sounds perfect, doesn't it? There was just one tiny problem. The guys didn't know I was a girl! Sure I stood in line with the rest of the girls in my class, but the similarity stopped there. I was the true-blue tomboy in class, the one that knew who every guy's crush was, the one who knew every secret, and the one whom most girls hated.

Not that I didn't love my life, I had two best friends, both boys of course, and spent every moment possible with them, much to my teachers' chagrin. I'd been pulled up by the teachers more times than I could remember for spending too much time with the boys. I had half a mind to tell the ladies not to bother as the boys thought me to be one of their own! My parents did get the brunt of this; PTA meetings used to revolve around my misplaced sense of belonging and the pranks which invariably came along with it, while my best friends got glowing records!

Moral: So long as you study well, you can get away with murder.

Since my best friends knew who the latest love of my life was, they would spend hours on plotting exactly how to embarrass me in front of him … which succeeded most times! One such time was when I was playing volleyball with the boys and *he* was the captain of our team. I managed to rescue a particularly difficult ball and he turned to me and said: 'Nice save'. And there I was a puddle of chocolate and melting by the second. For the rest of the day, my best friends said those two words so many times, I could've kicked their backsides blue. No wait, I think I did!

And at that time, if someone had told me that this 'tomboyishness' was just a passing phase and that I'd eventually grow out of it, I would've scoffed at them and hi-fived the nearest guy! But that's exactly what happened. All of a sudden, the guys were paying a lot more attention to the girls in the class. I was not their centre of attention anymore. The girls were blossoming into young women while I was left struggling with my puppy fat! (I still am, till date!)

And then one fine day, *he* came up to me and said he wanted to talk to me. My heart was beating fast, I was hoping he couldn't hear it. This was the moment I was waiting for. Even before he opened his mouth, I'd had two children with him! And then he told me he had a crush on one of those pretty little things. He wanted me to mediate and set things up for them. I was shattered. But again, the best part of being a teenager is that you move on.

I took exactly a day to cry and sob to my mother and to my two best friends. Ma told me not to fret too much over it and that there were plenty of boys left! The guys tried to help me, making me laugh by imitating the 'train-wreck' expression I had when I came back to give them the news.

I did survive, only to 'fall in love' within five days again! I never realised 'the-new-he' was crush material till that moment! What a waste of time! And there I was walking away into the sunset yet again, while ignoring my friends' grumbling at my idiocy.

But I did start to change, slowly, but surely. Maybe that first heartbreak does leave its mark somewhere. When I met one of my best friends after a gap of two years, I was well on my way towards becoming a girl! I'd grown out my boy cut into a ponytail, I wore pretty clothes, but the puppy fat stayed on! Some things never change! And when he saw me, he said, 'Wow ... okay ... so you look different.' That was possibly his way of accepting the changes.

Till date, all my best friends from school still have trouble accepting me as a girl! Years later, it took one man to see me as I am, and I ended up marrying him before he saw me through their eyes!

Moral: There is a sunset waiting for you, out there!

Ranjani Rengarajan Deoras

Clearing Love ...

November 2008

It's been eight years now since I opened this old trunk. While clearing it up today I found an old card. A Valentine's Day card. I had managed to pen down something on the card, but didn't have the nerve to give it to the person it was bought for.

October 1999

I was practising for the annual day function when I heard my favourite track by the Backstreet Boys being played in the adjoining room. I peeped through a hole in the partition but the singer's back was turned towards me, and the only thing I could see was a wonderful head of bouncy hair shaking to the rhythm of *Shape of My Heart.*

Finally I succeeded in seeing the singer in the assembly hall next morning. For some strange reason, I couldn't take my eyes off him.

During English class one day, I saw him pass by my classroom. Though I love Shakespeare, that day I couldn't concentrate on the sonnet Miss Kaya was teaching. I kept on gazing out of the window, waiting for him to pass by my class again. I really liked looking at him.

I even waited at the bus stop and let a number of buses pass by just to be with him for some more time. I don't know why, but even he waited at the bus stop till I got onto a bus.

'He is two years older than you, lives in Tollygung and yes, he sings quite well.'

'Why the hell are you telling me all this?' I was shocked when Armaan gave me the information. 'Ah! As if I hadn't noticed you looking at him. Anyway, the least you can do is buy me a choco bar for this data.'

'Push off,' I replied, exasperated at being so obvious.

But I still kept on gaping at him when he wasn't looking and I would still wait to catch a glimpse of him when he went by my class. Though I don't think he ever caught me staring at him, some of my friends did. On being questioned, I confessed, 'I think I am in love with him.' They felt he was aware of the fact that I looked at him; that he always stood in a position that made it easier for me to look at him!

Come March, we were writing our respective exams. On the second day, his seat was next to mine. 'Hey, can you lend me a pen?' It was the first time he had spoken to me. I was jubilant and the incident kept replaying in my mind.

'Who's that boy staring at you?' My mother asked me at the bus stop that day. During exams she would always come to pick me up from school.

'Who?'

'That tall boy. He seems older, which class is he in?'

'Oh him? I don't know. Some senior, may be in the eleventh.'

But I couldn't study that evening. 'Mom, are you sure he

was staring at me?' She looked at me from the kitchen and smiled.

'What happened?' I asked.

'Nothing.'

Time passed; the new semester began. There were new classes, a new curriculum and new students. Among them was Aaleya. She was everything I was not, and maybe that's why within a month she had befriended him. Some said they were going around, but a few also said that she made advances towards him but he ignored them. I didn't know what to believe.

When the rumors became rampant, I stopped looking in his direction. In due course of time a year flew by and it was time to bid goodbye to our friends at school.

It was the last day of school and my only chance to let him know how I felt. I gathered all the courage I could summon and went to school with a Valentine's card.

'You wanted to talk?'

'Yes, I did.' I paused. 'I wanted to say that … that ….'

'Say what?'

'Say that … that you still have the pen you borrowed last year.'

'That's it?' Did he seem disappointed?

'Avantika, that pen is very lucky for me. I want to write all my papers with it.'

'Okay then. All the best for the exams, do well!'

'You too.'

I didn't say anything more. I don't know why. I came back home and buried the card in this old trunk.

****

I have to clear the thoughts in my mind which have gathered dust like the childhood memorabilia contained in this trunk. Just like I need to make space in the house to accommodate guests who are attending my wedding next month, I have to make space in my heart for my fiancé. I have wondered a million times what would have been my fate had I confessed that day. I wasn't completely a grown up, nor was I a child. I was mature enough to be in love, but too immature to reveal it. After all, I was just sixteen.

The time for closure has come. I close my eyes, erase the past, put my mind to rest, no questions, just one simple answer. I love my fiancé and look forward to a new life with him.

Avantika Debnath

Me Too

Around a dozen odd friends had formed a clique when I was in the tenth grade. I was, of course, a part of it and so were Risha and Auryan. Teacher's Day celebrations were on in full swing and we were all dressed in traditional clothes. I noticed Auryan staring at Risha with unguarded appreciation; he'd obviously seen her only in uniform before and today she was looking gorgeous in a sari. It didn't take long to figure out that he liked her. Risha was unaware though; I pretended not to notice either.

The next day, Auryan sat next to me in the canteen and asked me casually, 'Risha hails from Lucknow, right?' I looked around nonchalantly and replied, 'Hmmm.' He was a bit miffed, but persistent. 'So is she going around with someone?'

'I don't know. She seems the studious kind,' I replied and walked off before he could get anymore information from me.

Over the next few days I had fun just watching them. The more he tried to hide his interest, the more apparent it was. I stifled a giggle as I let Devi (another friend in our group) in, on the goings on. 'What's wrong with Auryan?' Risha asked Suman, referring to his silly behaviour. Devi and I exchanged knowing grins, much amused with Auryan pendulating between getting to know more about Risha and pretending to be indifferent, while Risha was getting more and more baffled by his conduct.

'Everyone seems to be going around with someone or the other these days.'

I nodded at Auryan's remark while concentrating on sipping my cola.

'Risha is a nice girl. What say, Avni?' I didn't answer. But during recess I asked Risha if she'd ever had a boyfriend. She said 'no', adding she wouldn't have minded, but she had never met anyone she liked.

'And, if I say someone really likes you, then?' Her curiosity was piqued and she asked me who it was. When I told her she seemed sceptical. But then asked me what I thought of him.

On the way home, I related my conversation with Risha to Auryan. 'So what was your reply to her question?' Auryan enquired. 'I couldn't say anything. Sir noticed us talking and separated us.' I noticed his puzzled expression before I turned my face away to hide a smile.

'Anyway, forget it! I am not all that interested. Friends would make fun of me if they knew that I have started liking someone.'

Auryan never brought up the topic again and I wasn't mature enough to understand that he was acting disinterested to camouflage his deep feelings and the fear of rejection.

'I think she likes him too, but has backed off because Auryan is acting weird,' said Devi and I couldn't agree with her more. We both thought it was time to take matters in our hands. It was to happen sooner than we had imagined.

Not so long after, my teacher asked me to prepare a play for our Annual Day. I got my chance to play cupid. I chose

Devi as my partner and we decided to write a script with Risha and Auryan as the lead pair. It was quite a job getting them to agree to play the lead; nevertheless they conceded and reluctantly learned their lines.

The day before the show, during recess, the two were left alone at the basketball ground for rehearsals, while the rest of us peeped through our classroom window. Only a few minutes into rehearsals, Risha ran back to class and screamed, 'This is not fair! He forgot his lines. I was all set to say, "me too". But he just jumbled up all the words. I don't know how we can perform tomorrow!'

'Avni, I am sorry, I messed up your work,' Auryan said, following close on her heels. Recess was still on and we were trying to finish our homework. He went towards Risha and held her hand, trying to complete the rehearsal … or so we thought ….

'Avni's lines were great, but her script had words that I couldn't understand. All I want to tell you in simple English is that I really like you. I am an average student. Maybe I will keep on liking you when I am in college, and when I am working and even after that. When I get a job, I will propose to you. As of now, will you be my girlfriend? I really, really like you.' Without waiting for her cue she replied, 'Me too.' Though Auryan had not said a single one of his lines from the play, to my utter delight Risha said hers perfectly.

Needless to say the play was a hit and the lead couple is going steady, even after seven years. We are all waiting for them to get married and have our fingers crossed, hopeful that this time Auryan won't need 'divine intervention'.

Avantika Debnath

Netravati Express

July 20, 2010. I was at a railway station situated in Thrissur, the culturally rich city of God's own country, Kerala. From that day onwards, the Netravati Express would come to mean something special to me. For those who travel frequently by long distance trains, especially Keralites, this would be a familiar train. That day, the train was on time: 1.05 p.m. With chattering passengers, coach S10 was filled with warmth and stories of those who had been mere strangers till that day.

Sitting near the window, I watched the green meadows pass by. As the breeze kissed my cheeks, I thought of him. With the rattling sound of the engine, I hummed one of my favourite songs … *Ek din aap yun humko mil jayenge … yeh socha na tha …* But, why was I singing when I was not supposed to think about him. He did not care about me — he hadn't even called me.

Boarding the train the day before, I had been very excited with the mere thought of meeting him. I knew him from the way he talked and his behaviour, but I hadn't seen him yet. Was it just a teenage crush? This thought made me shiver. His words, 'I want to share my life with you and make you my life partner' made me believe that he loved me. Hearing his voice every day on the phone and getting regular emails had kept my love going for him. But one day, a few months back, I'd got the shock of my life ....

At home in Mumbai, I got up in the morning only to find that he had not tried to call or message me as he usually did. I called him on his cell but heard only the computerised voice saying that the subscriber was not answering. I messaged him again but there was no reply.

I left for work. I was a trainee journalist for a leading newspaper and the quest for finding stories kept me busy till noon. Once I reached office, the first thing I did was to check email, but there was still no reply from him. A small wave of fear engulfed me. Still I stayed calm, telling myself that he might be busy. As I typed the story for the day, my mind wavered in the midst of a sea of negative thoughts. All the feelings I had shared till now with him — was it all a prank? Was he gone? Would I never hear his voice again?

My distraught appearance made my colleagues enquire about my well-being. I decided to be discreet, as otherwise the questions posed would be many. Some would laugh, a few would ask whether I was mad to love a person whom I had never seen, and many would advise that I was on the wrong path. There would only be a handful who could have understood me.

But that day, after trying for about the twenty-fifth time, I was really tense. It was too much for me to bear. I sent him a mail again, a bit rude this time. Leaving the office, I did not go home but loitered in a park for more than an hour.

As I was crossing the road, the phone rang ... *Aao na*

… I was so happy; it was the most welcoming sound I could imagine. Standing there in the middle of the road, I started to cry. I took the call; his voice had the same love which made me smile through my tears. He explained that he had forgotten to take his phone with him and had been held up in an official meeting. I wanted to shout at him, but I was happy to hear his voice which dissipated all my tension and fury.

Thinking of the incident still gives me goose bumps. That day I made him promise that he would call or message whenever he was held up. But it was the same again, that day! I was travelling all the way from Mumbai to Kerala just for him; it was already twelve hours and I hadn't received any call from him.

I had planned the trip to attend an interview with a publication in Kerala. It was my parents' wish that I should shift to our native place, but more than that, it was for him that I was going there. The last time I had heard his voice was the day before, at eight in the night. He was at a party with his friends in Bangalore, where he had gone for a two-day official visit.

Now It was 1.20 p.m. and I had given up all hope. Somewhere, it seemed, I had been overestimating things or he was not interested in seeing me. At 4 p.m. I would reach my destination, Kayamkulam. Talking to him would be quite impossible from my grandma's place; he was aware of that. As the train chugged out of Thrissur station, I slowly started turning the pages of my novel. After about five minutes, I received the biggest shock of my life. I could not believe my eyes — a tall man was standing in front of me, staring at me. I knew him, I had seen this face somewhere, but he was still a stranger. He smiled, came forward and sat down next to me. I could not recover from my shock; this was the same face I saw in my mails and as a display picture on my computer screen every day. It was him. I couldn't believe my eyes.

He had proved me wrong. The guy now sitting next to me made me realise true love and its depth, which was more than what I could have imagined. It was a superb idea, planned by him, and executed with the help of his friends. I sat speechless. I had no words to describe how I felt.

But he just smiled and said, 'See, I came to see you first. Aakhir dulha hi toh aake dulhaniya ko le jata hai na? If I had a ring in my hand, I would have made you mine right away.' I could do nothing but smile. I was dumbstruck at this glimpse of his true love.

It's been three years now, but I still blush when I remember that day.

Suchithra Pillai

The First Butterflies

It was the feeling that Reeti would, for times to come, always associate with the enormous butterflies in her stomach and the happy buzz in her head. It was the day Reeti, a sixteen-year-old had her first tryst with that feeling called 'love'.

'Reets, hurry along now. If we're late for the debate today, we might not be allowed to enter the school campus, you know,' said Prianka, who was Reeti's team mate for their inter-school debate. Reeti was as laidback as they came. She loved anything to do with oratory and had established herself as one of the most vivacious and smart speakers in school. Reeti, in her most nonchalant tone, exclaimed, 'Yes Pri, we shall make it in time. Besides the main event got over yesterday,' with a flick of her hair.

Miraculously, they reached the venue on time and got the best seats in the auditorium before all other students flocked in. One moment the seat next to Reeti was empty and the next, her eyes fell on this tall, charming boy who had occupied the seat adjacent to hers. Call it the twist of fate if you may, but Uday, the boy next to her decided to break the ice with Reeti, beginning with, 'I couldn't help but notice a copy of *Shantaram* in your hand. Are you a fan of Gregory David Roberts like me?' And that one moment was all it took for Reeti to feel the sweet autumn breeze in the sweltering heat of Delhi. It was like this big bubble was suddenly inside her and she could not keep herself from turning a vivid shade of scarlet.

It only got better from there. Uday would make the lamest joke and Reeti smiled a smile that was wide, even by her standards. Reeti suddenly realised she wanted to know all about football and Uday could not stop telling her about his football team's exploits. Uday told Reeti that Nirvana was his favourite rock band, to which Reeti piped in, 'Oh that's funny. Nirvana is my favourite too.' Group activities had been organised for debaters on that day. It was not difficult to see how Reeti had eyes only for Uday and how everything that he said on any topic impressed Reeti like they were words no short of an epiphany.

Prianka decided that she was hungry and insisted that Reeti join her for lunch. It was not difficult to gauge that Reeti was in no mood to eat; it was as if her stomach was suddenly cast with a sheet of iron. Secretly, Reeti was hoping that Uday would ask her to accompany him for lunch and that brought a smile to her lips. 'Hey, lunch time! Can't keep my friend waiting any longer,' Uday said with the ease of someone who had definitely not considered asking Reeti for lunch. Feeling thoroughly rejected, Reeti went out to seek solace in Prianka's cheerful company and joined her for lunch. Needless to say, throughout lunch Reeti kept on stealing glances at Uday.

Lunch got over; and Reeti, woebegone as she was, bid goodbye to all the new friends she had made during the debate and was stepping out with Prianka, when she heard someone shout out her name from a distance. She froze in her tracks because there was no mistaking that voice.

'Reeti, were you actually going to leave without swapping email addresses with me?' Uday shouted between taking gulps of air, panting from running across the auditorium.

It was as if Christmas had come early. Reeti instantly knew this unmistakable feeling. She scribbled her email address on a napkin that Uday managed to find just then; he did the same. As they returned back to school, Reeti and Prianka could not stop giggling in excitement. 'You will mail him, won't you?' Prianka asked Reeti in hushed tones. Reeti only smiled.

The very next day she sat in front of her computer, beaming ear to ear as she began typing out an email to Uday. She had recognised the feeling — the feeling of falling in love as a teenager. It has been five years since then and the emails, phone calls and visits have not stopped. Teenage love does outlive its name sometimes, I guess.

Shreya Kalra

The Magic of Belief

In school, I had many classmates to interact with, but just one or two friends. Friendships never happened quickly with me and even if they did, they always remained superficial and never transformed into the usual fun-loving teen companionships that every girl dreams of. I never knew whether it was my fault or I was simply unlucky. Whatever might have been the reason, people simply made me feel shy and I kept my distance from them.

I had become too judgmental and blamed myself for this attitude. Deep down, I rebuked myself for not being a good student or excelling at any extra-curricular activities, which made one eligible to become part of the intellectual brigade I fancied at school. It took me a long time, until finally I met someone who made me realise that I could be appreciated simply for what I was.

We had shifted to this newly-built house. Life was getting tough for me. I only had a handful of friends and now all of a sudden I had to do without them. I was a nervous wreck with very little hope or courage to make new friends all over again. Though apprehensive, I did make a start with the ones around our new home.

Just after a week, I was invited to a friend's birthday party, where I came across this boy. It was 1994. Though we were in the same school, I had never talked to him before though I had caught a few glimpses of him at school. He was quite popular with his friends and teachers. Being good in studies and extra-curricular activities always made him the topic of discussion everywhere. In addition to that, his extremely outgoing and friendly nature made him no less than an iconic figure.

He lived just a couple of blocks away from my place and we used to share the same school auto. Things were subdued till we started talking more frequently just a week after our first meeting. This time sparks flew....

I had never known anybody before then who would take care of me just like my parents did. He was fiercely protective of me. I could feel it. He pushed me to get ahead in life, in all the endeavours I believed in. He started giving me lessons in subjects I wasn't good at, refusing to believe that I would not be able to grasp them.

His patience and belief in me did wonders! I started to become more confident about myself and also worked hard, in order to make him feel proud of me. Since he had the attributes I lacked, I always feared the prospect of losing my cherished world with him. It was a blend of emotions which made me fight and improvise in many areas over the next few years. His faith in me grew leaps and bounds and consequently, I had more people around me who loved and appreciated me. And I had started appreciating myself as well.

Things were just fine till he proposed to me one fine day. I was shocked. I had just started cherishing this new-found friendship when a confusing term like 'love' was thrown at me. Love had no meaning for me other than short-time flings, for which I had very little inclination. I wanted him to be my friend, like he had always been. The entire episode left me more confused and scared — confused as to what should be my stand and scared at the possibility of spoiling everything and losing him!

I had no other friend to talk with, so I decided to discuss it with the person concerned. Like a true friend, he listened patiently, empathising with my fear and confusion. He calmed me down and said that he would wait, as he knew his belief would make it work, some day. However, he did not pressurise me for anything and we remained the best of friends.

After school, I was sent to college, miles away from home, where I realised I was missing not just my family but also him. I remember how I tried to stay in touch with him every day and yes, he reciprocated my efforts. Be it emails (which were then just becoming popular), letters or phone calls; we did everything to keep our magic alive. And yes, the magic worked.

I was glad. He gave me time, much more than I had imagined. He was there with me like a true friend, guiding me through life and making me a better person each day. My entire persona had changed for the better. People who ignored me earlier had actually started taking notice of me. In fact, over the next few years I noticed that they had started looking at me as someone special. Nonetheless, deep down I knew that it was not magic, but the belief of someone, who I realised had now become more than a friend.

I finally understood that it was better to marry one's best friend rather than go for an arranged marriage. Most Indian middle-class parents think the idea of love marriage is taboo. However, it never mattered to me, especially, when I realised that my childhood friend was perfect for me. I fought hard, because I knew my life with him would improve, not just for me but even for my family.

We fought against all odds and won. I am glad I married him and it has been more than a year of marital bliss. Life is fun now. I have never been happier — it is like a dream come true! Some people say the magic ends after marriage, but when he looks at me I know it's still there and will be for the rest of my life. Maybe because now, even he knows that I have started to see and believe in the magic of it.

Malavika Roy

3

ON FRIENDSHIP

The only way to have a friend is to be one.
–Ralph Waldo Emerson

A Friend in Need

I think I liked Kalpana almost instantaneously when I met her along with another friend in my junior college days. Whenever I remember those days, a sense of satisfaction and happiness fills me. So innocent, naive and lovely were those moments! Whenever I go down memory lane, the enthusiasm and eagerness of our teen days come alive, giving me the zeal to move on.

My friendship with Kalpana grew stronger after our first meeting. I admired her patience and she liked my enthusiasm. We started cycling to college together and would merrily chatter, giggle and enjoy our rides.

As our Twelfth Board exams were approaching, we soon started studying together. Surprisingly, we never discussed each other's problems, but slowly, we began to understand each other's sorrows, likings and fantasies. Lazy days were replaced by hard work since we had to really slog for the twelfth exams. I think I was the more ambitious one and made her also work hard with me, while her patience helped me stay grounded.

After the results came, we both realised that we had to now go our separate ways. We had got admission in different engineering colleges. However, our friendship kept growing despite the separation. We kept in touch; I enjoyed writing to her about the various avenues opening up before me, and would wait impatiently for the postman to deliver me her letter. I had got admission in the four-year degree course, while she was in a five-year one. Therefore, when I got a job just near the town where she was staying, we were both overjoyed. She would often come down from her hostel to spend the weekends with me.

Unaware of what destiny had in store for me, I was enjoying my life. I got through the UPSC exams and was extremely elated. After all, I was a Class I officer now! However, my flights of fancy were soon brought to a grinding halt as the news of my father being hospitalised reached me. Those days, we had no mobile phones. I had gone out with my batchmates, and when I came back, the professor at my training institute gave me the sad news. As I packed my suitcase and rushed to the station at midnight, I wondered who would be taking care of my father. My mother had left with my sister for her medical entrance exams and my younger brother had gone to my uncle's place to spend his holidays.

When I reached home next morning, I saw Kalpana's father along with one of my father's friends, attending to him. My father was in a coma, it was sad to see him lying there like a statue on the hospital bed. At times, the doctors would say that he would survive and was slowly getting better. At other times, suddenly some complications would develop. There was also an underlying worry in my mind as to how I would be able to support my family. My brother was ten years younger to me, my sister eight years my junior.

They had not even begun their higher education. I was also new in my job.

But again I had my friend Kalpana with me and she was a tower of strength. She would not let me or my mother cook during the entire duration of my father's hospital stay. She would get packed meals for all of us. There would be no words of advice, no false hopes and no opinions — just her silent presence. She would hold my hands, pat my back and reassure me that she was always there for me. I would be reassured by her presence and she did not fail me even once.

My father expired after twenty days of struggle. I felt drained out and blank. A lot of relatives and friends had gathered, but Kalpana was somehow missing during those days. But, as soon as they had left, she was again there with me — giving me the confidence that helped me tide over this crises.

Fifteen years down the line, I am happily married and well-settled; my siblings have also done quite well and my mother keeps hopping merrily from one child to the other. Kalpana and I live quite far apart for us to meet very often, but I know that whenever I need a friend to share my happiness or a shoulder to cry upon, she will always be there for me. Similarly, I know that if she ever calls me, I will go running to her. It is something that took root between us in our teen years and has continued to grow stronger ever since ....

Neelam Chandra

A Mismatch but Still a Match ...

When I joined college in Chennai, my hometown, I was depressed because I missed my hostel friends from school terribly. When I met Siri, I knew she was the friend I needed. She was an eternally happy soul, reprimanding me whenever I took to sulking (which I did a lot). 'You have a fleet of cars, a mansion, a wardrobe overflowing with designer wear; why don't you appreciate the kindness god has bestowed on you. Most of us can only dream of a life like yours,' she would say.

My answer was always the same — being away from friends whom I had grown with and loved made me crave for them. A friend mattered more to me than a ride in a chartered plane.

Though we got along famously from the very first day, Siri's behaviour towards me was always a little strange. She came from a middle class Tamil family and I belonged to a privileged Marwari one. She believed that the difference in our monetary status would eventually be the bone of contention between us; I cited examples of people with different social standings who were the best of friends. We were completely opposites; I was the quiet one, she was peppy; my conversations were guarded as I always tried to be politically correct and she always spoke her mind. She was the talker, I the listener, and I loved the equation we shared.

Siri loved her independence and whenever I tried to extend whatever help I could, instead of feeling close, it seemed to offend her.

In the holidays I joined a baking class. I wanted Siri to be the first one to taste the cake I had baked. I sent it to her place but she sent it right back. I was angry, hurt and frustrated. I found her attitude ridiculous and thought that perhaps she was right. We could never be good friends.

The next three days went without a call from either end. On the fourth day she called me. I was cold on the phone and she asked me, 'What is wrong?' I told her it was nothing. It was then that I heard her softly sobbing and she said that she had returned the cake only because she had no way to reciprocate all the favours that I had been showering on her.

I knew then that I had to get her to see how I felt. 'Siri,' I said, 'I understand how you feel but you see when I baked that cake, I wanted you, my best friend, to taste it. When it is raining outside and college gets over, I want to drop you home not to flaunt my money but to protect you from catching a cold, and I would do it for anyone and definitely for my best friend because I care for her.' And then I too began to cry.

After a few minutes spent sobbing, Siri said she saw my point and apologised.

Siri now lives in Chicago with her family, and I in Pune with mine. Our husbands know that we have to speak to each other every day or else ....

Our friendship has withstood all tests, be it time or distance and emerged a winner.

Arti Sonthalia

Dawn at Dusk

'Guys, what are you thinking? Are you all nuts? How could you enter the class just after boozing? If you are caught, all of you will be suspended! Or worse!' I shouted at the top of my voice to my friends. Those guys had some guts coming to the class drunk! As I don't drink, I was left behind, more often so nowadays.

Class started, and in less than five minutes, Raj got up and loudly muttered something that no one understood and then sat down. I doubt he himself would have understood; the guy was high on alcohol. The Professor turned his attention to him but I managed to divert him by asking some silly questions. 'That was close, someone make him shut up!' I whispered to my friends. Raj was my best friend and I always covered for him whenever he was in trouble.

Raj stood up again, and this time the Professor saw him. Next second, Raj was nowhere to be seen. I bent down to see what was happening and there he was on the floor, throwing up. This is one time I can't bail him out, I thought. Soon the whole gang was caught. I was spared as I was not drunk and had a good reputation.

Veer, the silent guy in the class, came and sat next to me, and enquired about what had happened. When I told him, he said, 'You keep your head out of this, man, they deserve it. Moreover if you get involved, your reputation will be spoilt. And those guys aren't worth the trouble; they are not as trustworthy as you believe them to be. Bad company, dude, I'm telling you. For once, listen to me.'

'But they are my friends, and they need me most now,' I said.

The college initiated an enquiry for the incident. Soon I was standing outside the enquiry room. My friends were all waiting for the investigation to begin and were relieved to see me. I told them that I would talk to the enquiry officers and request them to be lenient. I knew the staff, thanks to an English speech I had once made. I decided to use my good reputation to bail them out.

By the time I came out, I had been successful in making the officers agree with me.

'You can be very persuasive! But it won't work another time with us,' the officer said as I left the room.

'Just go in and tell them the truth. Apologise and say that you won't repeat it. I have taken care of the rest.' All of them thanked me and I then left as I had to meet the Principal.

But I was called urgently by the enquiry officer out of the meeting; I felt something was wrong. When I went to the enquiry room, none of my friends were to be seen. They must have got away, especially after my recommendation, I thought. Little did I know that something totally unexpected was waiting for me ....

'We cannot let you get away with everything you do, can we?' commented the enquiry officer.

'Pardon Sir, what do you mean? I really don't understand.'

'All your friends have testified against you. Just because you are in our good books doesn't mean that you can take us for granted, young man.' My head started to spin, I couldn't understand what was happening. 'Could you please explain, Sir?'

'They have testified that you convinced them to drink in the morning and then brought them to college by assuring them that whatever goes wrong, you will step in and save them from trouble since you know most of the people here. You have proved to be a greater disappointment than anyone else. You don't deserve all this fame and reputation. You are misusing it and I will see that you are put in your rightful place.'

My whole world started spinning as he began talking. Betrayed? By my own friends, whom I thought to be my world? That was something I couldn't digest at all. Everything started to get dark, and I fainted.

I woke up in the health care ward and found the officer sitting next to me. I recalled what had happened and started to speak, but he cut me off and said, 'I'm sorry, kid. I shouldn't have doubted you, but their story was so convincing. They got what was coming to them. Perhaps more, as they tried to pin it on you.'

'I still don't understand, Sir. What happened?' I asked. 'I thought all your friends were rotten company. But now I see that you have some true friends — it is so rare to find in today's world. You should be very thankful to Veer. If not for him, you would have been suspended. He is really a good person.'

'But what did he say, Sir?'

'The truth. That you had nothing to do with their drinking and you did not know they were drunk till they were in class. And also you tried to save them voluntarily, but you were bitterly misused. Veer was waiting outside to meet me when you were pleading for your friends, he had heard them plotting against you. He couldn't tell you right away, but he hurried to me as soon as he heard that you fainted.'

The next day I was sitting with Veer as my so-called 'friends' were suspended. 'Thanks man, I can't thank you enough. I should have listened to you in the first place.'

'Told you they were bad company,' he grinned.

Friendship with him was a really different experience. The most intriguing trait in Veer was that he never asked anything from me. Nor about me or about what happened in the past. Nothing! When I confided in him, he listened. After that experience, this new friendship was really refreshing.

Initially I thought he might turn out like others, but he has proved me wrong in every aspect. He is reliable, trustworthy, caring and has brought a real change in my life. He has taught me to trust again. I may not have been always there for him but he's always there for me.

Kamalesh Babu J.

Friend, Philosopher and Guide

'You guys are so familiar with each other, it's almost as if you have known one another practically forever!' But actually they had known each other only since a year. A close friend remarked, 'I've known you, Liz, all my life, and you've become closer to him!' Ajay was something of an outsider, but Liz obviously liked him a lot for they spent considerable time together.

They were the best of friends; they sat together in the bus to college, in the same classroom, did their assignments together, studied together at home, chose the same electives, were often lab partners, and could quite often be found together in the canteen too.

Most of us were involved in the usual teen pastimes, and didn't find much time to ponder on the activities of others. But we did sometimes wonder about them. For all her intimacy with the rest of us girls, Liz never discussed Ajay. All we knew was that he lived in a neighbouring locality, with his father and brother. We also knew his mother had died some years ago. Ajay was studious, and determined about going far in life. He was quiet, polite and rarely ventured out. Very different from the guys we knew.

Of course, such a friendship was bound to attract attention. Liz and Ajay's unusual affinity did set quite a few tongues wagging. They were the butt of many coarse jokes. There was even a Professor who bluntly asked Ajay if they were going 'to make a match of it'.

Once there was an uproar in class when a classmate made a very loud and particularly nasty comment about them. The rest of us were righteously indignant; Ajay only glared at his tormentor in mute contempt. But Liz was sitting beside me; and I saw the pain flash across her face, and heard her agonised whisper 'I wish they'd leave us alone!' I caught a glimpse of the binding friendship that stayed strong in spite of the callousness and occasional narrow-minded cruelty of youth.

As more romantic and interesting relationships blossomed among our classmates, the interest in Liz and Ajay faded, barring sporadic insinuations when the class mood was particularly raucous.

The four years of college soon came to an end. Ajay graduated at the top of our class, with Liz close behind. And in a whirl of activities involving GRE, TOFEL and campus interviews, we realised that our years together were now finally behind us.

The very last day was spent in organising a farewell party. There was plenty of food, and plenty of saccharine songs playing on everlasting friendship. There were many rather soppy speeches; by then most of us were on an emotional high. We were surprised to see Ajay walk up to the podium. Ajay as a rule reserved his oratory skills to technical debates and seminars, so we were rather agog to hear the class recluse speak.

Ajay began just like the others — a rather hasty narrative of how enjoyable college had proved to be, and went on to relate his future plans (MS in the United States, of course). But when he said, 'All of you have spoken about friends — so I'm going to do so, too. But unlike most of you, I'm not a member of any gang.' The whole audience went so silent one could almost hear the proverbial pin drop. 'Eliza and I aren't in love, engaged, married or in any other way paired up together. He took a deep breath, and continued, 'I don't know how many of you are aware of this — but my mother passed away quite a few years ago. I've completed school since then, joined college, made acquaintances, laughed and joked, but the black hole in my heart remained — a void of despair, until I met Eliza.'

'I know most of you've wondered about the relationship between us. I'll tell you now. Eliza is my friend, the best friend I'll ever have. If it hadn't been for Eliza's desperate attempts to pull me back from my personal hell, if it hadn't been for her support in studies, both mentally and sometimes financially, if it hadn't been for her friendship, sympathy and understanding — I never could have gone through college — she's my friend, philosopher and guide.'

Ajay's voice broke by the end of his speech and we were all in tears, and he almost fled down the podium, to his place of refuge — near Liz.

Well, it's been many years since we parted. We all got jobs, some went abroad like Ajay and some are in India like Liz. I've no doubt that their respective spouses and children mean the world to them.

But Liz and Ajay's friendship always stood out as a testimony that love and friendship can take different forms. They validated my belief that you could remain 'good friends' even if the world scoffs at it. This is my tribute to their friendship.

Gayathri Povannan

Friends

It was my first visit to Delhi after we had moved to Singapore. I was very excited and called my best friend, Alina, to arrange a sleepover at her house. In anticipation I packed a bunch of things she would like to see during our sleepover — stuff from my new life in Singapore, some memorabilia I was certain she would love to revisit ... and many, many pictures.

I would die of embarrassment if anybody other than her ever saw some of the pictures. Alina had been my best friend for years before I had to move. It was like we were joined at the hip and though she wasn't as funny and interesting as some of my other friends, she was the one I knew I could talk to about anything — school, boys or books. We decided to meet the day after my arrival as I had to spend some time with my grandmother before that.

The day I landed in Delhi, Alina called to ask me if another girl, Shruti, could hang out with us till around 8 p.m. I was slightly hurt because we would be meeting after ages and I had so much to tell her. I couldn't obviously talk to her with this 'Shruti' character around. But I figured it would be alright as we would probably only talk seriously at night. Despite being a teensy bit put-off, I looked forward to my time with Alina.

We met the next day. Shruti and I did not quite hit it off and it was only my love for Alina that stopped me from strangling her. We even started fighting about who was Alina's best friend — though it sounds childish now when I write about it. Apparently Alina had told her that they were 'best friends', and when we asked her for a clarification, Alina chose not to reply and changed the topic. We spent the rest of the time watching movies and doing whatever Shruti thought would be fun. Nobody even bothered to ask me for my opinion. I decided to sulk and wait until Shruti left, before asking Alina what was going on.

When Shruti finally did leave, Alina suddenly became quiet and said that she was sleepy (after having been quite energetic till a few moments ago!). We went to sleep early, without talking much. When I left the next morning, Alina didn't even bother to drop me off till the parking lot.

I felt hurt and angry with her for having replaced me with a new best friend but then I told myself that I could do without friends like her. How I wished that I had found another new friend before her so she would have been the one to feel hurt and lonely. Why was it that I had never replaced her even though it would have made staying in Singapore a whole lot easier and fun? I felt like retaliating by acting indifferently to her betrayal and compelling her to think that I had never really liked her that much to begin with. But the truth was that I felt scared to be without a best friend. I was desperate and didn't think I could live without one.

When I returned to Singapore, I stumbled on a piece of paper lying on my desk. It had been there since my new friend Tanika had come over. She had been doodling with these new calligraphy pens I had got and had written our names together with 'Friends Forever' scribbled at the bottom of the sheet. I called her up and waited for her to answer the phone.

'Hi! Are you back? I missed you so much!' she yelled excitedly. Suddenly the vacuum inside me vanished. 'I was thinking, let's go shopping today, we could buy these really cool friendship magnet bracelets I saw at Accessorize the other day and then we could spend the rest of the day doing fun things ...' she continued. I felt overjoyed. The words 'best' seemed just like a tag after all and what mattered most was the wonderful word 'friend'!

Inika Sharma

Friends Indeed

I entered my French class; it was dark and quiet except for the rustling of the crisp autumn leaves outside the classroom. It was a 'make-up' exam and only two of us were appearing for it as we had missed the actual exam due to illness.

None of my friends would be around during this exam and I realised how much I missed the familiar faces. I had never crossed this gate alone; we were always hanging out together — laughing, teasing, shouting at one another and making plans. French was always a big struggle for me and on top of this, I was all alone today. A chilly gust of wind entered the room and I shivered as I sat down on the cold desk.

I glanced nervously through my notes. It was the final exam and I was nervous. The other candidate walked in. 'Hey, don't look so worried,' she remarked. 'The exam won't be as difficult as you imagine.' She ruffled my hair and took her seat.

'What is wrong with me? So what if I am alone this time? I have spent two hours here, three days a week, for the last one year!' I thought to myself. But what actually troubled me was that none of my friends had even bothered to wish me luck!

The Professor entered the class and asked me to pick up a topic for the oral exam and start preparing. I collected my belongings, picked a chit from a bowl and settled in a chair at the café. I must mention that our French institute had excellent classrooms and a lovely café.

There was a lot of noise coming from the garden outside the café. I was trying to prepare a speech on the topic for my oral exam but couldn't concentrate because of the racket. 'Aditi, go tell those people not to make so much noise,' said my Professor, sensing my discomfort. With a sullen face I went out intending to yell at the group.

As soon as I stepped out, I was dumbfounded. I blinked my eyes in disbelief. 'Surprrriseee!!' they shouted in unison. My friends! They had it all planned. They were waiting there for me to finish my exam after which we would all go for a movie. My Professor stood at the doorway of the café and smiled. She, too, was a part of the plan!

I was delighted and miraculously all my anxiety vanished. I sailed through the paper and obtained a staggering eighty-six per cent.

I had always known it, but that day I was convinced that my friends meant a lot to me and I too mattered to them. The feeling of emotional security that comes from having good friends, can help us tide over all troubles with ease!

Aditi Parikh

Funny Valentine

The final exams at school loomed large on the horizon. The teen excuse of 'combined study' to hang out was being used prolifically.

My teachers had noticed the slump in my grades. I was no longer among the students lined up for prizes. As Miss Framji, our algebra teacher put it, my parents could not tell why, but I was happy that I was doing just enough to get by. Doordarshan would telecast *Top of the Pops* for one hour every week and once I got hooked to songs like *Rock and Roll' Gypsy* and others, dates and numbers from my books disappeared from my head to be replaced by *I just called to say I love you* and other lyrics.

Study holidays for the ICSE exams had begun. For me, it was not 'study' but 'holiday' that was the key focus. During the holidays, the only thing that I missed was our life outside the classroom and the school bus route 166 filled with young Lochinvars, little Lolitas, talks of leaked question papers and laugh-a-minute pranks. Emma, my very romantic classmate, was also my neighbour and we decided to study together.

Every morning, trips to a nearby chapel became the norm; I prayed for good results while Emma wished for her many crushes to blossom into reality. She had one major crush on a tall Anglo-Indian boy called Valentine, who played the guitar and charmed the girls. He looked like Elvis Presley and his signature song was *Wanderer*. Emma never tuned into the story of his life that was apparent from the songs he sang: ... *'I'm the kind of guy who never settles down ...'* He would sit near the door of his house and sing loudly for every girl who passed by. But Emma of course thought that Elvis only sang for her.

So our study holidays became a research project on Valentine. We listened to old songs together. Emma read innumerable Mills & Boons, where she imagined herself as Jonquil, the heroine and Valentine became Jaden. I stuck to the classics and decided to turn into a heroine who never succumbed. (Of course all this was done in the free time we allotted ourselves during study time!) We then decided to put the project to the test on one of our days off from studies.

After dressing Emma like a bride and me as the bridesmaid, we went for Sunday mass to actually find out if Valentine liked Emma. Our strategy was that while Emma kept her head down demurely and prayed, I would have to steadily look at Val to see if he was showing any interest by glancing in Emma's direction. This ritual went on a couple of times till one Sunday Valentine caught me alone and came up to say rather harshly, 'Hey, Specsy (thanks to the glasses I wore) stop looking at me, I don't like you at all.' I was appalled, died a thousand deaths and told Emma she was to blame for my humiliation.

The holidays got over, exams flew by, results came out, and I had not performed in keeping with the expectations of my parents and teachers. Although I was offered a seat in the Science department in college, I took up Arts (not even Commerce!) and continued with the determination that I would do well academically but never compromise on life outside the classroom.

Life went on. I was now working in a advertising agency. One day on my way to work where I had a deadline to meet, my moped ran out of petrol. It was also the last day to submit an application for a study course I was doing simultaneously. I thought I would have a fit.

As I waited for divine intervention, a matador van stopped and a much older-looking Elvis popped out exclaiming, 'Hey Specsy, what happened to your glasses and what's up?' Taken by surprise, I decided this was not the time for verbal vitriol, so I told him of my predicament. In a trice he hauled my moped and myself into his van, drove me to a petrol station, got my moped filled and asked me to hurry off to work.

Later, I went to his house to thank him and told him all about Emma and our school girl nonsense, and that I was not the one with the glorious crush on him. We soon became really good friends. He would always agree to play music for the childrens' programmes I organised on the radio. He was quite a child at heart — gentlemanly and chivalrous in an irreverent, unorthodox manner.

He came for my wedding and in his gung-ho style said, 'Can I give away the bride?' but I was already in the pandal, so I told him that it was not possible since the rituals were over and that I'd already been 'given away'. We both laughed at our craziness.

We lost touch with each other later on, but if I ever bump into him, it'll be like *yesterday once more*. He will say rude, cheeky things to me, and wait for my counter witticisms. I would like to tell him *shine on, you crazy diamond*, because he's that — a diamond in the rough.

Madhuri Jagadeesh

God Could Not be Everywhere, So He Made Friends

We were about to set off on a school trip to Nargol, specially arranged for us, the sixth graders. We were about eighty students. We were divided into two groups and given the keys to our rooms. The next day we were asked to form groups of seven. I was the captain and I chose my class gang or to be more specific, 'The Pop Stars'. I chose Nishi, Aenasha, Pyusha, Vikeshi, Yashvi, Ami and myself. We had to compete with other groups to prove that we were the best.

We had lots of fun preparing for the exciting activities our teachers had arranged for us. We had to act out the meanings of the names of our groups, advertise for 'Smile Toothpaste', and we even had a rugby match. We, The Pop Stars, were strong in our minds, but physically we were small and fragile. The game was new to all of us; Yashvi and me were the only sports persons in the team. We had to compete with a team that was stronger than us, but we did not lose hope.

As we took our place in the playground, the opponents shot us disparaging looks; they were definitely more confident and though we were scared, we tried to stay calm and cool. The referee blew his whistle and the game started. We had a good start and, as the game progressed, in frustration the other team turned aggressive.

I had the ball and was a few metres away from the goal post so I ran as fast as possible. A girl named Kenil hit me hard on my back and tried to twist my neck. She literally sat on me to snatch the ball. I let go of the ball and lay on the dusty field, my eyes filling with tears. My friends rushed towards me, they picked me up and took me aside. I saw tears in Nishi's and Aenasha's eyes. My other friends surrounded me, clutching my hand, trying to console me. The wound was mine, but they were feeling the pain too. Feeling much better, I was back on the field the very next minute.

As if by magic my pain vanished, and even today I marvel at that incident ... I actually felt no physical pain at all! I had known that doctors heal; that day I was convinced that love heals faster and miraculously.

God could not be everywhere, so he created mothers and mothers could not be everywhere so God created friends. Friendship is a special gift, so treasure it and never take your friends for granted.

Akanksha Singh

Moving On

I look at you playing with her hair
It kills me,
I just stand and stare.

My mind recreates images,
And they seem to haunt me,
I see myself in those arms,
Those hands caressing my hair.

You see me looking and you walk over,
You smile, and I gaze in wonder
I see the twinkle in your eyes,
I notice the curve of your lips,
And remember the feel on mine.

My heart beats louder
My knees start to shake
I feel tears brewing
But I display a smile …
Wish I could tell you how I feel
The ache in my heart doesn't seem to heal.

I feel my friend tugging on my skirt
The warmth as her hand slips into mine
I run, but I feel her close behind.

I throw myself into her arms,
Let the feelings flow
didn't say a word but I know she understood
She held me in her arms and told me I could.

She was my pillar of strength
And helped me move on.
Guys come and go I realised that day
But best friends are here to stay.

Vedika Chitnis

My Best Friend

We live on the same street. We are neighbours and close friends. However, everything else is different about Shreya and me. I am tiny and she looks a bit mature for her age. I can keep on talking for twenty-four hours, whereas she is quiet and composed. Our tastes hardly match!

We have known each other since we were in class seven. Though we studied in different schools, we shared the same syllabus. We enjoyed doing our homework together. Gossiping was the biggest glue that bound us together; we used to talk about everything under the sun and lent a patient ear to each other as well. It does not matter how nice and understanding parents are — there are some things that you can share with only your friends, like copying in exams! For me, Shreya is the one.

We passed high school and higher secondary school with our friendship growing in leaps and bounds. We entered college; she took up engineering and I opted for dentistry.

This increased the range of our conversations; we had different colleges, different subjects, different friends, so there was a lot to chat about always. Then finally, a cloudy sky began to hover above our street ....

You always see it in the movies. You go to college, there is this big building and vivacity is in the air. Bunking classes, wearing unconventional clothes and finding someone to court tops the list. As for us, we waited until we stepped into college to open our feathers in those directions.

I met Harsh. I told Shreya about him. Shreya met him but she did not like him. She remarked that he was crude and I found that comment really rude. This incident gradually created a gap between us. In a month or so, we were hardly talking to each other anymore.

My craze for Harsh faded soon but the intimacy with Shreya seemed to have been lost.

Time really slips by fast. Months passed. We walked the same streets daily, but never saw each other. I missed her a lot but never called. There were no grudges any more, no tangles, yet I could not bring myself to call her.

One fine Sunday evening, I heard the doorbell ring. My dad opened the door but I could not hear any voices.

'Strange,' I thought. I called out, 'Daddy?' No answer! I went up to the door to check what had happened. There was my father sitting on a chair and Shreya was standing at the door.

'Hi,' I said. She did not say a word. I gestured her to come to my room. She did not respond at first but then slowly came towards me, held my hand and then tied a band around my wrist. My wrist was so thin, she had to wound the ribbon twice over! But why was she doing this?

And then I remembered, it was Friendship Day!

The most amazing thing about human behaviour is that at times, in a fraction of seconds, one can experience multiple feelings. I was afraid that my eyes would well up with tears but then I saw that she was already crying. We do not belong to the generation that cries at the drop of a hat, we are the cool ones, but ... do tears know that?

We hugged each other and sobbed for a few more minutes. My dad quietly left the room, guessing that we had much to talk about.

We are again the same — talking, talking, talking. At times I wonder, what if I didn't have Shreya and I shudder at the thought.

Mudra Rawal

My Friend Spartan

It was my second anniversary with my best friend, whom I call Spartan, as I think he belongs to another planet. Spartan is witty, funny, understanding, outspoken and immature. He is also a brat at times, pulling my leg and also gently pointing out areas where I need to improve myself. I expected he would plan something out of this world, memories which would make me smile, something to make me dream. Instead Spartan, true to his nature of springing odd surprises, took me on a trek. It was peak summer, forty-two degrees; I was not into trekking and shamefully out of shape.

'That is why we need to go. You need to lose some weight,' he muttered as a matter of fact. Diplomacy was not one of Spartan's qualities and I had learnt to like him for that. So as I huffed and puffed up the mountain, Spartan nimbly climbed as if it was child's play. We had carried nothing to eat or drink. So here I was — tired, hungry, thirsty and mad at my friend and his strange choices.

There was a deserted fort on top, and as he merrily related its history, oblivious to my troubles, I wanted to strangle him. He had not even wished me on our anniversary, to add insult to injury. As I cursed him on my way down, Spartan sprinted dwon, singing all the way. I was so angry; I just wanted to go home. He dropped me off without a word. It was the most horrible anniversary I ever had.

In the evening, the doorbell rang and Spartan stood outside with his silly idiotic grin and a big bouquet of white roses (I had told him I loved white roses; and he seemed to have remembered). He had come to take me out for dinner at a fancy restaurant on his brother's bike which he had borrowed for the occasion. The restaurant prices made my eyes pop.

'Spartan, this place is too expensive. Let's go,' I said. Spartan seemed unfazed. He had saved his allowance for weeks for this dinner. Then he said, 'Happy second anniversary. In the morning I put you through a terrible time but I never left your side. In the evening, dinner was pleasant and I am still with you. What I am trying to say is that I will stand by you through thick and thin. That is what friends are for.'

I knew then why Spartan, with all his quirks was my best friend; and why only he could pull off something as extreme as this to teach me that no matter what the situation in life, if you have true friends, the road somehow becomes easier.

Khursheed Dinshaw

Not Without You

There was a ripple of excitement in the classroom as the teacher handed out circulars and announced a school trip to Goa. We had just stepped into senior school and this trip would be the first one for us. The delight was palpable as everybody formed groups and started making plans.

It was impossible for us to concentrate on our studies for the rest of the day. No matter how hard the teachers tried to maintain silence, there was a constant buzz in the classroom.

Once school got over, nobody bothered to loiter around and make small talk, but rushed home to get the consent slip signed by parents. The trip was only eight days away and there was so much that had to be done!

The excitement continued the next day as everyone handed in the consent slips signed by their parents to the teacher; everybody except me. My father had refused to let me go for the trip. He had his reasons; I was recovering from a chronic ear infection and the ear had to be kept dry till it healed completely. I promised Dad that I would be cautious and would always wear a cap that covered my ears as well, before swimming, but he was adamant. Goa was all about water, he said and at present the weather there was rainy.

The doctor had warned that even a little bit of dampness inside the ear could be disastrous and my father was not ready to take a chance. We argued, I cried and there was a whole lot of drama, but his answer was still 'no'. There would be several such school trips, he reasoned. But for me, it was the end of the world.

I sat in a corner of the classroom and sulked, and all the animated conversation around me suddenly became unbearable. My friends were shocked. Their disappointment was evident as all their planning came to a complete halt. The four of us brooded while others rejoiced. My friends decided to opt out of the trip but I couldn't let that happen. That wouldn't be fair! Although a part of me secretly wished that they wouldn't go, I knew it wasn't right to feel this way and convinced them to carry on.

As the days passed, I came to terms with it although the feeling of being deprived lingered on. My friends too, couldn't contain themselves anymore and despite their efforts, their excitement would spill over in my presence, to which I would smile stoically and say, 'It's okay.'

Finally, it was the big day. Everybody had assembled in school to leave for the airport in a coach; everybody except me. The next four days would be holidays for me. I had never felt so dreadful about holidays before. With a heavy heart and teary eyes, I chose to stay confined in my room. It was 11.30 a.m. Their flight must have taken off, I thought. I buried my face in my pillow and wept ....

After about an hour my mother came to my room to call me for lunch. I refused but she was not ready to listen to me. She reprimanded me for behaving like a baby and asked me to come to the dining table immediately. As I reluctantly walked into the living room, I was stunned — my three best friends were sitting at the table, ready to have lunch!

'What are you doing here?' I shrieked in disbelief.

'Not without you, girl!' they shouted back and rushed to hug me. I broke down and sobbed. I was touched by their feelings for me and felt guilty too. But they assured me that they wouldn't have had any fun without me and that there would be many more such school trips in the future. We laughed, cried, had lunch and made plans for the next four days.

At that age, it is not easy to make sacrifices, but my friends proved that we shared a strong bond. Probably that is why it has been over two decades and we are still the best of friends!

Swati Rajgarhia

Of Distances and Friendships

'Posted out ...'

'Where?'

'Bangalore ...'

I had been wanting to visit Bangalore during my summer holidays for a long time now. I had fallen in love with the cosmopolitan city ever since my last visit. But now that we were posted there, it felt different. I was not as excited as I had hoped to be. The reason? Friends!

We had all known each other for a few months then. Some friendships were forged on the basketball court and some were renewals of older friendships.

All of us had got together around January. We were all in the same boat, faced with the challenge of Board exams and the imminent setback of soon losing touch with close friends from school. That kind of got us all together.

Though all of us had different and conflicting personalities, we attracted each other like magnets of opposing polarities. I was the fiery one, getting irritated at the smallest of things but almost immediately calming down. Always fighting and screaming, I was the spoilt brat.

'R' was the calm one. Less fiery, always poised and trying to get me to stop screaming on the road. I cannot describe her in mere words — she was a charmer, polite, hardworking, and the most diligent amongst us. But thank god, she did know how to have fun! She truly is a goddess of beauty.

'K' was the emotional one. He was always there for us. I had known him since my nursery days, which is when we were about four years old. So our friendship does go back a long way.

'A': words fail me when I attempt to describe him. I had known him for a few months when we were about ten-years-old and honestly, the experience hadn't been all that memorable. He used to irritate the heck out of me and still does. He has always been troublesome, as a ten-year-old putting snails in my cycle, or being an irritating neighbour, messing up my hair. Somewhere in between, I realised that I had found a very good friend in the same irritating guy.

With them, time had stopped for me. I could be the ten-year-old who whined at being teased and would be ignoring them when I knew that within the next five minutes, we would be laughing over something totally silly.

So naturally, leaving them behind was not something I was looking forward to. We made the most of the time left, though. We went for movies and watched DVDs at home. Basically, we made enough memories for rainy days.

I left for Bangalore and soon K and A also got transferred. So now we were all in four different places.

We did promise to keep in touch and it was easier during the vacations. As the new sessions started, it became more difficult since we all got caught up in our lives.

True friendship survives distance and we have had our times. We lose touch for some time, we have our misunderstandings, loneliness, feeling left out of the latest news, et al. Then, the phone rings and we are all together again. Sometimes they would comfort me as I confessed to being lonely, and sometimes I would be the comforter. But whatever the case, we always had each other.

We helped each other settle into our new surroundings. Their constant encouragement to find 'replacements' for themselves helped me settle in here with good friends. In each one of the new friends that I have made here, I find a little bit of them. It is a constant reminder of the best months of my life.

We plan to meet every year; this Christmas will mark our first meeting. It is the beginning of a set of new memories — the mark of a new beginning, refreshing an existing page, opening a new book to write in ….

Dikshita Maheshwar

Simple and Sensible

A real friend is one who walks in when the rest of the world walks out.

–Walter Winchell

The teen years are an important time of our lives, when we begin to experiment with the rapidly evolving outside world. My folks, just like all frantic parents, had a 'rule chart' for me. I had conveniently chosen to accept the 'agreeable' options, and decided that the more exciting and creative rules were meant to be broken. One such rule was that I make sensible friends. They believed that there was life beyond high school and it was vital to choose the right set of friends. They wanted me to stay away from the drama queens who they thought were obsessed with boys, and the 'eye candy' boys whose favourite diversion was to have a bevy of good-looking girls around them. Well, as much as I have would have liked to comply with my parents' rule book, I was sure this archaic rule was not meant for me.

I wanted to belong to the 'cool and happening' group in school — the exclusive group of boys and girls who set the latest trends for others to follow, created their own lingo, went out together and always did exciting stuff.

In the tenth grade, while preparing for our Board exams, we felt the heat because the curriculum was vast and because we never studied. I was confident of doing well in all subjects except maths. As our final exam was only two months away, I knew I had to make up for all the lost mathematics marks and the only way to do so was to do well in the surprise tests to be held in the forthcoming two months. But unfortunately, I came down with viral fever and could not attend school for a week.

A few days later, on a Friday afternoon, the doorbell rang and I saw Ravi standing there. Ravi was a short, bespectacled boy with oiled hair, who was popularly known as the 'whiz kid' of our school. We boarded the school bus from the same stop but had never exchanged any words. We were in the same section, something which I was unaware of till the day I was made to sit beside him (as a punishment), because I was chattering with my friends.

'Everyone in class was enquiring about you,' he said. I was taken aback.

'Thank you. I am fine and shall be back in school on Monday,' I replied.

'We have a maths exam on Monday,' he announced.

'What?' My voice was loud enough to wake up the whole neighbourhood, which generally went into a snooze mode during the afternoons.

'Yes. There will be a test on Algebra and Trigonometry.' Before I could react, Ravi turned and walked out.

For the next hour, I drowned myself in my Maths book, but nothing went into my head that was full of twisted cerebrum and cerebellums. I was sure the fear of a Math exam was enough to catapult my body temperature up once more.

The door bell rang and it was Ravi once again. What more did he have to say? I was furious. 'I have got the Algebra notes that you missed. If you want I can stay back and help you. It's not as tough as you make it out to be,' he said.

I looked at him gratefully, and invited him inside. We studied till 8 p.m. I was exhausted but Ravi patiently tutored me and sorted out my concepts. My mother made sure that Ravi was treated to delectable homemade snacks and chocolates. It was only when Ravi's mother called for the third time, did he leave for home. The next day was a Saturday and he arrived at 10 a.m. We both spent hours working out mathematical problems, with occasional breaks for food and television. Finally, by Sunday evening we were able to finish our revision.

As Ravi was leaving, he stopped at the doorway and took out a pen from his case. 'Here, take it. This is my lucky pen, which I use to write my exam papers. Tomorrow I think you need it more than me.' I was moved and thanked him for his kind gesture.

The next day when we reached school, I walked with Ravi to our class. I could see my friends gazing at me with astonishment. An oiled hair 'whiz kid' with me, the 'cool and happening' girl? But strangely, 'cool and happening' didn't matter to me any more.

My exam went off rather well and for the first time my math teacher praised my performance. That night I called Ravi home for dinner. He had become my parent's favourite boy and now, he is my favourite too.

My grades kept improving and so did my friendship with Ravi. Over the years he taught me to be sensible and smart while dealing with complex situations. After all, friendship is not about pointing out our weaknesses, but finding ways to get over them. And over the years, I've been so grateful for my simple and sensible friend.

Abhilasha Agarwal

Taj Mahal of Friendship

It was my thirteenth birthday the next day. I was really excited and wanted to invite all my friends for my party. The boys who played with me were mostly the kids of high-ranking IAS officers, but there were some children of the mess employees too. Anil and Santosh were the sons of helpers in the mess, but they were brilliant soccer players and good friends of mine.

My invitation cards were yet to be distributed. I hurriedly started scribbling their names on the cards. When it came to Anil and Santosh, I was confused. I wasn't sure if I would be allowed to invite them. I asked my father who agreed without any hesitation. Wow! I remember jumping with excitement and breaking the chair! But it didn't matter. I was allowed to invite everyone. What a wonderful birthday party it would be now. With the cards in my hand, I raced to the ground and found all my friends gathered there. I distributed the cards with pleasure.

My birthday party had been organised at the Police Officers Mess. It was huge and there was lot of place for us to play. I had promised Santosh and Anil that I would pick them up from the playground as they had no conveyance.

When I reached, they were ready and waiting for me. I was surprised to see a small gift in Santosh's hand. He hugged me, wished me and gave me the gift that was from both of them.

The party was a great success. My parents paid special attention to Anil and Santosh, and tried to make them comfortable. Even my school friends mingled with them without any qualms.

After the party was over, it was time to open the presents. I was eager to find out what Santosh and Anil had gifted me. When I opened their gift, I found myself speechless. It was a small model of the Taj Mahal in a plastic case, with 'Best Friends' written on it.

I immediately took the model and placed it in our drawing room, amongst souvenirs brought by my parents from all over the world. It was the Taj Mahal of Friendship!

Anhad Mishra

That's What Friends Are For

Ujwala and Tina were neighbours in our colony. They used to attend the same school and travel in the same school bus. But these two proud teenagers were sworn enemies. They were leaders of different houses at school, and during competitions, in the class or on the playground, they played like bitter rivals. Whoever won, gloated at the other's defeat. Whoever was vanquished, plotted and planned for the next fight.

Ujwala and Tina's parents were good friends and could never understand the animosity between their children.

'Why aren't you friendly with Tina?' Ujwala's mother would ask. 'Are you jealous of her? She's such a well-mannered, loving child. You could learn from her behaviour.' Ujwala used to make a face. 'She's haughty and proud and thinks she's God's gift to the world. I have many good friends, Ma, and I don't need another.'

Likewise, Tina's mother berated her daughter. 'I don't understand why you girls can't be friends. Ujwala is a lovely child — always polite and respectful. People in the colony have begun to comment on your behaviour. You must make up with her.'

'Leave me alone, Mother. I have enough good friends. I don't have to run after Ujwala,' said Tina and walked out in a huff. The children's park was empty. She sat on a swing and rocked back and forth, thinking angrily about her first run-in with Ujwala.

Both their fathers were retired Army officers. One was a Major General and the other was a Colonel. It was Tina's thirteenth birthday and her mother had presented her a beautiful dress. Tina was the centre of attention in school that day in her fine birthday dress. Her classmates said she looked like a lovely fairy. Tina went around distributing Cadbury bars to her classmates. But Ujwala refused the chocolate and stomped off, saying loudly, 'She's only a Colonel's daughter but she behaves as though he is the Field Marshall himself.'

Tina retaliated. 'I'm proud to be a Colonel's daughter, especially when he is a highly decorated one.' She knew exactly why Ujwala was riled — she distributed only éclair each time on her birthdays.

'And that's how everything began,' Tina mused. 'She started it. So why should I go and make friends with her? To be insulted again?'

In their last year at school, they played a hockey match against another school. Tina and Ujwala had to play in the same team. They were overjoyed when they routed their opponents. Soon after, everyone left for home. Tina had forgotten her pen in the locker room and rushed to get it. She was shocked to find Ujwala sitting on the floor, holding her leg and crying in pain.

'Oh, my God! Ujwala, what has happened to you?' Tina cried out.

Tina saw a huge swelling above Ujwala's left ankle. Someone must have hit her hard with a hockey stick during the game. But despite the pain, Ujwala had played to the finish.

'Can you walk?'

'It's really painful. But if you help me I can limp to the gate.' Leaning on Tina's arm, she hobbled to the gate, groaning with each step. But the school bus had already left.

'Sit here,' Tina said, pointing to a large stone, 'I'll go find an auto rickshaw.'

That was the beginning of the thaw in their turbulent relationship, and Ujwala's mother couldn't believe her eyes when she saw Tina helping her daughter home. Ujwala had to stay away from school for several days, and Tina surprisingly felt her absence.

'Without her around, life is really dull,' she thought, 'I hope her leg heals fast.'

Tina visited her on a couple of occasions, taking story books for her to read. 'Here, these books will help you pass the time.'

But their friendship really took off a few months later when Tina had to accompany her parents to Delhi for a fortnight. She had adopted a small stray dog that sneaked into the colony every day. It was a cuddly white puppy with black ears, one of which always stood upright.

'Stop feeding this stray,' Tina's mother scolded. 'Here we are trying to eliminate these animals from our colony and you keep fussing over one.'

But Tina had made it her business to feed it once a day and cuddle it for a while. Now that she was going away for a fortnight, she was worried. Most of her friends in the colony refused to help out.

'I can't do it. My mother would throw a fit' said one girl.

'It's a stray. Could be dangerous,' said another.

Ujwala heard about it.

'I'll feed the dog, Tina,' she offered. 'Just tell me when he comes and what you give him to eat.'

'Thank you so much, and don't forget to give him a cuddle,' Tina beamed.

'My pleasure, Tina,' Ujwala said, 'After all, that's what friends are for!'

The two lovely girls had finally realised they had so much love to share.

Eva Bell

To Be a Good Pal ...

I nervously held the water bottle in my hand and said goodbye to my father. It was my first day in the seventh grade of a new school. I walked to my classroom and sat on one of the unoccupied seats.

A girl entered the class and sat beside me. 'Umm, what's your name?' I asked her mustering up some courage. 'I am Monika, the monitor of this class ... and hey, just so you know, if you talk or misbehave in class, I will have to give your name to the teacher!' Monika said and walked away. The tiny bit of confidence which I had gathered inside me, vanished on hearing her words. Four classes went by in a haze after which I tagged along with the girls towards the assembly hall during recess.

I sat quietly, dreaming of my old friends and old school where I belonged. This place was alien. Suddenly, a girl's voice interrupted my reverie. 'Hey, you look lost. Don't worry, next year you will be sitting here with us, having fun and telling this to another new girl!' She introduced herself as Natasha.

Natasha was godsend; she briefed me about the school, the other girls and all the teachers. She talked to me for a while and then introduced me to her best friends — Priyanka and Aisha. Days went by and I slowly made several new friends.

Soon I was comfortable and having a great time. A year later, I found myself shoving others out of my way to reach the eighth grade classroom. As I sat down, the memories of my first day in school flashed across my mind.

After a while, next to me, I heard someone murmur, 'I am so lost!' I turned around to see a new face staring at me with wide, fearful eyes. 'Hey what's your name?' I asked. 'Anaisha. I hope it's okay if I sit here?' she asked.

'Oh, it's totally cool … and don't worry, you might be feeling lost now but I am sure, next year, you'll be sitting here with us, telling this to another new girl. Anaisha, your name means "unique" right?' I said, trying to help her feel comfortable.

'Yeah, it does and thanks … I already feel better.' Anaisha said. 'Hmm … let's see how you feel when you meet the others in recess; we are a naughty lot …' I said, with a wink.

This scenario repeated itself year after year. Every new girl came in feeling lost and we welcomed them with comforting words. It is easier to make a new girl feel comfortable than to be mean to her.

Teenage years are the best years of one's life and friends make it even better. Today, as I put my arm around Natasha, my best friend, and walk through the school corridors, I feel grateful for having a pal like her who taught me to be a good friend to others.

Manushi Desai

I'll Wait ...

I'd always thought that friendship was like glass, once broken, it could not be returned to its earlier state. But I was proved wrong.

We were best friends. We took care to never hurt each other. And Nupur always envied this bond between us. Nupur was a spoilt brat who wanted all the boys to like her and all the girls to follow her. Unfortunately she was a very good friend of Shamini, my best friend. I always told Shamini to be careful when she was with Nupur because I found Shamini to be easily swayed by her. Nupur had a strong influence on her; she forced Shamini to stalk the guys she liked. With the passage of time, Shamini's bonding with Nupur became stronger and her feelings towards me became lukewarm. I was very annoyed and started ignoring her. We could no longer be called best friends, or even friends.

Two weeks before the mid-term examinations, everyone was busy with some serious studies but I was down with severe bronchitis. I still went to school to attend some important revision classes. But I had high fever,was barely able to speak, and overcome, I buried my head in my face while tears rolled down my eyes. The pain had become unbearable.

Shamini saw me crying in pain and quickly took me to the sick room. While everyone was busy studying and copying notes, Shamini came to see me after every period and would sigh in relief when she saw me fast asleep! She fed me during the lunch break from her own lunch box (she hated parting with her food!) and helped me to the bus when school got over.

She was like my Florence Nightingale that day. I had got my best friend back.

But my happiness was shortlived. Shamini would be leaving the school soon, she was going away. I was heartbroken. I tried to smile, but ended up crying. I sat in the corner of my room, as memories flashed through my mind: about the sleepovers, parties and all the madness we had enjoyed. I was going to miss her. I cursed God for this. If He had to separate us, why did He draw us so close to each other? My life would never be the same. I was happy about one thing though; changing schools had been completely her decision. No one had forced her to make the choice.

After this year's reshuffling we were in different classes, but after every bell, we rushed out of our classes to see each other. We would try and meet as often as possible. It was December and Annual Day rehearsals were on in full swing. This was actually the time when we could bunk classes and so I would meet her often to spend the last few days with her. Days passed. The Annual Day preparations came to an end. We had our final exams in one month after which the semester would get over. Soon exams too got over; it was her last day in school.

Everybody gathered around her during dispersal and started wishing her luck for the future. 'Keep writing mails',

'Stay in touch', 'We'll stay connected through Facebook', everybody screamed. Unable to control my tears, I ran towards her and hugged her.

The school buses had started to leave and disappointed that we had hardly got time to say a proper goodbye, we ran to our respective buses with tears in our eyes. I never got a chance to thank her for all that she had done for me.

We would meet every weekend and talk on the phone every day. But things have changed. Sometimes she would be too tired to call or would be busy during weekends. The gap between us gradually widened. I can sense the distance between us but I'm going to give her the benefit of the doubt. She has been there with me in good and bad times. When I thought our friendship was broken, she proved me wrong. I'm going to wait for her because I know one thing for sure; even though time fades away memories and I have other friends, none of them can fill her shoes.

True friends are hard to find, difficult to leave and impossible to forget.

Rashi Agarwal

4

IN TOUGH TIMES

Life's challenges are not supposed to paralyze you; they're supposed to help you discover who you are.

–Bernice Johnson Reagon

Boyfriend

When we were five, didn't we have a whole lot of boys who were our friends? And now, we get nervous even just talking to one!

In school, the easiest way to become popular was to have a boyfriend. I found it rather stupid. I mean, my best friend was a boy and it didn't really matter to me that he was physically different from me. Why was I supposed to feel shy around him like my girlfriends did? The boyfriend craze was like a plague, spreading all over school. Towards the end of the Seventh Standard, all my friends had boyfriends. They weren't exactly drop-dead handsome; in fact most of them were average looking with acne and facial hair.

To my amazement, my best friend Vinay, suddenly started acting weird around me. He would often ignore me and had even stopped calling me at home. It was tough trying to figure out what was wrong with him, amidst running from one tuition class to another.

One fine day, I received a letter from a boy that read 'I love you!' I was stunned and flattered at the same time. Despite Vinay's inexplicable behaviour, I decided to talk to him about it. To my surprise, Vinay got furious and bashed up that poor boy. What was wrong with him? Exams were around the corner and I decided to stay focused on them rather than think about Vinay.

Soon after our exams, Vinay gave me another shocker. He asked me if I would be his girlfriend! I was bewildered and thought it would be best to ignore him for the next few months. My friends thought I was being a fool to let go of a cute guy like Vinay. Finally, I gave in to peer pressure and consented. We were a 'couple.' But it was so awkward saying 'I love you' to each other and holding hands. It felt peculiar calling him my boyfriend and addressing him as 'sweetie' or 'baby' (the worst were the meaningless anniversaries!).

The truth was that I was just in love with the feeling of being in love, not Vinay. I confessed to Vinay, and mercifully, he understood and we decided to part.

I was effectively getting over my first break-up with less tears and more sympathy from my friends. Vinay and I succeeded in remaining good friends, putting an end to the entire series of 'first love' and 'first break-up' as swiftly as it could be!

Drishti Chawla

Bridging Distances

Even now, as I roam these empty streets
Bouts of nostalgia jab at me,
I remember as little girls, we'd made promises together
Of being Best Friends Forever.

It was cruel of fate to do us apart,
And cruel it was that I couldn't see,
But then you did choose them over me
Striving to achieve what you never were,
Nor could ever be ...

But, some things are best left unsaid, they say,
And so we did, long time back; part and go one's way.
No more seizure causing phone bills,
No more jumping off window sills,

No pleading with teachers to let us sit together in class,
Gosh! We drifted away so fast.
I see you every now and then,
In school corridors, between classes,

And for girls who were once best friends,
We don't even make eye contact amongst the masses.

But in heart of hearts I do,
Miss you a lot and hope, so do you
Even though Anna says 'it's never too late for bridging distances,'
I can't help but wonder …

Do you still remember those instances?
Those countless sleepovers, where no one slept much,
'Coz of makeovers, scary movies and popcorn to munch.
All the kicking and pushing in swimming lessons,
Calling up the other for comfort, before dentist's sessions.

And now here I stand, trying to make amends for both of us,
Praying silently, that you won't snub me or laugh at all the fuss,
Made over what is now long forgotten,
As I walk up to you, I hope soon the distance would shorten …

I see you standing in the market with your friends,
I guess, gossiping or discussing the latest trends,
I take a deep breath and step towards you,
And as I call out your name …

I see you turn around, look at me and pause,
And then finally, hurriedly make your way across,

I also see the look of pleasant surprise change
Into the shock and horror that flit across your face,
As a speeding car sends you flying into the air

Not the screeching of brakes nor the terrified screams
Wake me from the sudden terrible dream
And now as I sit in the hospital that has declared you dead,
A cold sense of dread and loss turns me to lead
Through tears that threaten to last forever
I watch our parents grieve together.
And I can't help but wonder
Did you still remember those instances?
And why was I so late in bridging distances ...

Harshita Bartwal

Everything Would Be Okay

She stared out into the black sky,
To empty her brain of thoughts,
Trying not to look back.

She reaches out in pain,
Numbness
She wants to embrace …
Help her, free her,
Be her saving grace …

She picks up the blade,
Puts it to her hand,
It looks like a scar a lethal weapon would make …
Her head spins at the sight of red,
She feels faint, numb …
A little pain at the back of her head.

She stumbles up to stand,
She can't see …

Blinded by tears from the pain in her hand …
She washes it and puts on band aid,
Making it look like it never happened,
Into that category she just did not fit …

She put on kohl and some gloss too,
And a smile to finish it off …
No one saw the tears in her eyes, blue.
Her friends crowded around her,
Asking where she had disappeared,
She waved it off with a shrug, staring at the ground …

She wished they'd just understand,
What she was going through,
Without her telling them the truth …
She looked at him, willing him to catch her eye,
Willing him to realise the pain she was going through,
After he said the last goodbye …

But, maybe
It was time to move on,
To stop harming herself for him,
To live her life being strong …
She hadn't given up ever,
And she wasn't planning on doing so now.

She knew it would be really tough,
Moving on, away from him,
But she had to go on, even when it got really rough …

She knew, that whether he'd go or stay,
She trusted herself now,
Everything would be okay …

Sneha Tulsian

I Forgive You, Daddy

The cool refreshing northern winds blow in from the mountains, ushering in pleasant sounds as the crystal chimes hanging on my window strike against each other. I wake up, hands folded in prayer, for blessings to shower upon my precious siblings, my mom and ... err ... daddy too .... Then with the whistle of the water boiling in the kettle, as usual the head of the family wakes the three lazy creatures with her 'it's time to wake up' line.

In my home, my mother is the head because after her divorce, she had to take up all responsibilities. Two years after the divorce, I joined a residential school, and every second Saturday my mother, along with my brother or sister, would visit me. Every Friday night before the second Saturday, I would tuck myself under the blanket and start my descent into depression. Deep inside, I felt intense hatred, questions unanswered and anger building up. The first man in my life had left me without even watching me take my first two steps. I would curse my existence as I wet the entire pillow. I would recollect what my mother had told me about Dad. Even at the time of my birth, Dad was nowhere near her; he was a drunkard and a drug addict. He would stay out late with other women and would disappear often, sometimes nearly for a month. Dad created one problems after the other and separation was the only way out for them.

Now, I'm super glad that at least he has changed his life … he is a pastor now, married to a doctor with four kids. I know now that Dad belongs to someone else and he will never come back to us.

In the hostel, I always avoided the topic of family with my friends. My heart was consumed with jealousy at their picture-perfect families and their praises for their 'hero' fathers. They would talk about what their fathers had promised them if they stood first in exams. I had first-class grades but all I got was a kiss from Mom. But Mom has had her share of tears and she is the strongest lady I've ever seen, my two-in-one parent. She never makes us feel neglected. She would come every second Saturday with a bountiful smile, but something still seemed missing, which always made me wonder if I could ever forgive my father.

One day, the entire hall was decorated for an important occasion, Father's Day. I felt out of place; I entered the bathroom and wept out of hatred for my father, but somewhere deep down I realised that I still loved him.

Somehow, I gathered courage and sat with my friends for the programme. The Warden announced that everyone was welcome to come forward and talk about their fathers. I was stuck to my chair like glue. Then I saw my friend, Pansy, going forward — she was in tears as she spoke about her late father and how she wished he was alive. We prayed as a group for her. Suddenly I heard a small voice deep down inside me saying, 'Don't you want to forgive your Dad, let go of the bitterness and start off afresh?' I felt peace inside me and the hatred was replaced with love. I went and hugged Pansy, my friend. I realised it's never too late and despite of his wrong-doings, he is a human being who needs forgiveness.

I ran to the Warden filled with tears as I pleaded with her to allow me to use her phone. She readily agreed and I called my Dad. His voice made me shed more tears, I simply couldn't express myself. I just muttered, 'I love you Dad, I forgive you Daddy.' On the other side my Dad was saying, 'I've been praying hard for this day when I'd receive forgiveness.' I felt a huge load taken off my shoulders. I realised life has a lot to teach us. Forgiveness is the answer to mend a broken relationship.

Lhouvina Angami

Kiss and Go

There comes a time in your life when you are so much in love that nothing else matters. All that your Mom has warned you about, all the principles that meant so much to you go up in smoke. Only, the person in front of you matters. And your feelings for him.

I nearly died when it happened to me. The situation overpowered me when my boyfriend held me in his arms. We had been intimate before but never overtly so. My instinct told me this time it was different. Was I ready for this level of commitment? My doubts were totally directed towards my inner self. He had gone on his knees and proposed marriage multiple times. Marriage was an eventuality for us. I stopped my active brain from questioning too much and decided to follow my heart instead. I was nineteen and he was twenty two. We knew all about the birds and bees, of course. That was our moment. I was willing to let it change me any which way.

We lived in a typical cottage not uncommon in Darjeeling. One day when my parents were not home, the sudden appearance of my boyfriend at my door, when he should have been working, pleasantly surprised me. He was an employee of a nationalised bank. He had come to inform me that he was leaving for Kolkata the same evening as his mother urgently needed him to sign some documents.

This was the first time he was going to Kolkata in the two years we had been going steady. I clung to him for life. He hugged and kissed me. I experienced the rush of blood in my veins and saw stars with closed eyes. I come from a conservative family and in our community it is almost a crime to get close to a man before marriage. At the moment, I did not care ....

When he said, 'You know I love you, don't you?' all my inhibitions deserted me. When I nodded he added, 'I will never hurt you.' I hid my face in his white shirt. He kept speaking softly against my hair — love flew all around us until we surrendered to the moment. A door opened before us and we became new members of the lover's club.

A couple of weeks later, I was at the corner coffee shop on time. I was about to meet my boyfriend after his return from Kolkata. Varied emotions made me phone him impatiently. Finally he arrived and apologised for being late. But I did not care. I was ready to wait for him all my life.

Cutting into my romantic mood he informed me casually, 'I got engaged while in Kolkata. She is a nice girl. You know I only said "yes" because she reminded me of you; same skin — tone, height and voice.'

He not only broke my heart, he did it in a disgustful manner.

Is it possible to foresee a betrayal? I felt awful the entire week. How come it takes two individuals to build a relationship, but only one to break it? My dreams were five feet eleven inches in size; if I could wrap my arms around him all my dreams would fit in. Ignoring the dull pain at the back of my head I called him. I had to see him one last time to remember him in my nightmares.

He reached five minutes after I did — blue tees and faded jeans always made him look extra handsome. I stood up in reflex, leaving my coffee untouched. 'I will drop this handset (a gift from him) at your bank first thing tomorrow,' I said.

He looked hurt. 'Hell no, you keep it. It is yours. You know I am engaged, not married. I made myself very clear to Ma that I am not marrying for the next three years. Until then I'm yours. He sat down and sipped coffee from my mug but he already seemed like a stranger to me.

Wishing him a piece of the heartbreak that was going to be mine for a long time, I walked out leaving the mobile behind. My heart was broken but my dignity was intact. Some people wear their mask so well that it is not easy to see their true colours. I could have insulted him, but deep down I realised he was not worth it.

I realised then that when your family tells you to be careful, it is because they want to protect you and not because they want to stop you growing.

As told to Ghazala S. Hossain

So Beautiful

'She'll wake up soon enough,' said Sharmila aunty, Bibi's mother, smiling bleakly at me. 'Don't worry!'

We both glanced at Bibi, who lay there with her black curls on the pillow like the rays of the setting sun.

'She looks like Snow White,' I said, ignoring the saline tube that was attached to her arm.

'Yes, a Snow White who tried to write her own happily-ever-after story, all alone!' stated Sharmila aunty.

'Yes, but that's because her Prince Charming refused her,' I replied in her defense.

'You both are merely fifteen now, how do you know that your everyday Tom is a Prince Charming? And for that you let go of everything, Princesses? The King, Queen and the entire kingdom?'asked Sharmila aunty, as she left the room.

I remained silent. That was one thing I couldn't understand. Why suicide? My best friend Bibi....

My mother never lets me miss school. At times when I want to bunk school, I have to beg and plead with my mother. So, it came as a surprise when she barged into my room just as I was pulling up my navy colour school skirt and said, 'I think you might want to miss school today.'

Later, I came to know that Sharmila aunty had called us the previous night, just before dinner, to give us the shocking news that Bibi had swallowed about twenty sleeping pills. Aunty had a dinner meeting that had got cancelled so she had asked Bibi to dine with her. Bibi, as usual, had refused and they had a fight. Suddenly Bibi's words started getting mumbled, she lost her balance, and fainted.

Sharmila aunty called for a doctor immediately who understood the situation. Thankfully she was able to avoid police interrogation as the doctor sorted everything out in his clinic. By morning, he had Bibi back in the house. Sharmila aunty had acted quite mechanically throughout, but as morning crept in, she couldn't take it anymore. She had broken down and asked for me; someone whom her daughter was close to. She had requested me to come over, hoping I could help her to understand her daughter. 'Is it my fault?' she kept asking. 'Have I ignored her too much?'

But Bibi had gone beyond all explanations. Why would she take such a step? Was anything worth it? As she lay immune to the world, images of the times we had spent together came back. She was so much like me, yet so different. At one level I totally understood her, at another I had completely lost her. I gazed at her pale pink lips; we had bought a cherry lip gloss just the other day. That day we had also bought a bottle of vodka for the first time. I get butterflies in my stomach even now when I think of our little adventure.

The wine shop was flanked on either side by the children's park and a Mother Dairy booth. So, it was quite difficult for two underage girls to go and buy alcohol without the entire locality knowing about it. But Bibi, as usual, had a plan. 'Don't be a coward!' she had said, 'I have a fantastic plan.'

'What plan?' I enquired.

'A very good plan,' she replied with a twinkle in her eyes. 'See it's all about timing. When do you think is the best time to go?'

'Umm … after dark, when both the Mother Dairy booth and children's park have shut down?'

'Idiot! That's when Birju uncle, Moti bhaiya and almost everyone we know, visits the shop!'

'Then?'

'It's better we go at a time when everyone is sleeping and the Mother Dairy and the children's park is closed.'

'Night?'

'No, idiot! Afternoon!'

'But what if someone recognises us?'

'They won't, for we will be wearing costumes.'

'Costumes?'

'Yes!' she said and pulled out a black bundle from a green plastic packet. 'I have borrowed two black burkhas from Nazneen!'

'Wouldn't it be weird if two burkha-clad women go to buy wine in the middle of the afternoon?'

'Ya, but *we* won't be suspects!' she said with an air of triumph.

Thankfully, the two burkha-clad women who went to buy vodka at 3 o'clock on a Wednesday afternoon didn't shock anyone except for the lone wine seller. Bibi did all the talking, while I merely accompanied her. The butterflies in my stomach seemed to have become giant birds that were devouring me from the inside, and I relaxed only after we returned home.

And then, we laughed. How we laughed! Since no one

was home, our laughter echoed! Even that made us laugh. Bibi fell on the sofa with a thud and toppled over the vase that was kept on the side table. Usually we would have been scared or nervous if something like that happened, but there was no stopping us that day. We continued giggling. We would have surely had the vodka that day if we could have stopped giggling, but we couldn't. And we kept the vodka hidden in her closet for another day. But that another day didn't come soon enough.

The next day, when Bibi had gone to return the burkha to Nazneen, she had met her brother Tariq.

'It's love at first sight!' shrieked Bibi on the phone. But before she could elaborate, she got another call. 'It's him! I'll call you later.' But she didn't call, for the entire week. I was hurt, so I didn't call her back either. I quietly suffered the pain of her detachment and much to my mother's delight, got engrossed in my books. My teacher had noticed the sudden change in my usual self and had asked me if anything was wrong. I laughed it off. I lost my appetite and sleep but managed to keep myself distracted in the reality of books.

One fine day, Bibi messaged me, 'We kissed!' I didn't reply. The night she took the sleeping pills, she had messaged me, 'He said he can't marry a Hindu!' I ignored it. She was thinking of marriage and I didn't even know? She had completely removed me from her life, so what was the point in sending these little feeders? 'Why aren't you replying?' she messaged again. I hadn't replied to that either. So now, I couldn't help thinking whether it was partially my fault as well.

Time passed slowly. I kept gazing at my best friend. She

seemed to have no intention of waking up. I felt scared. Tears started swelling in my eyes. What if ...

Suddenly her eyes fluttered open and she stretched her arms. She then widened her eyes, sat up and asked, 'Why are you crying?' I couldn't reply. My happiness had stunned me to silence and tears kept rolling down my cheeks.

'Arrey, I'm sorry! Bad plan! But forget it, want to have the vodka?' She was glowing like the first rays of the sun. I hugged her tightly and my tears gave way to loud sobs. Sharmila aunty came in, held us both firmly and started crying too. Soon, Bibi too joined in — for a moment it was so beautiful, we were all crying, yet so happy and so very sorry.

Joie Bose Chatterjee

The Oystered Pearl

I'd spent the first twelve years of my life with a father who got drunk every other day. He used to flare up and get emotional. Mom was the one who had to face it all. But she was always calm. I never realised then what she had to go through. I'm sure it must have been a very difficult time for her. But I was at an age where I could not understand her too well.

We moved out of the house when I was about thirteen and took with us the few belongings that we could retrieve from the house. It took time but she managed to provide us with the necessities. We never spoke about Dad, but we always supported each other.

I often wondered what life would have been like if I still had him, but over time I discarded the thought. As the years passed by, I thought little of the matter.

Like every teenager, I changed too. I liked to keep to myself and didn't converse much with Mom. She understood that I was changing and adapted accordingly. She was a broad-minded person, but there was one thing that she always stressed on — though I was allowed to have male friends, I was not to get into a relationship.

I did not heed her words and thought her then to be narrow-minded. I am very determined and like to do what I think is best. Before I knew it, I was in a relationship at the age of sixteen. I didn't tell her about it. I felt happier than ever and I wished it would never end. One day, my boyfriend told me that his mother had found out about us and that we had to break up. I was shocked and hurt. I couldn't understand how he could break-off so easily, but I didn't say anything. I just accepted it.

It hurt a lot. My friends knew about the break–up but I didn't speak to them about it. I started keeping to myself and hardly spoke to anyone. I barely ate and the result was pretty evident. My family started getting concerned too. Mom knew I had lost someone but she waited for me to talk to her. She knew I wouldn't tell her if she asked.

I acted normal with my friends, Mom and even my ex-boyfriend. He was hurt himself and feeling guilty about it. I didn't want to put him under any more pressure. As a result, I was under a lot of stress; I couldn't find anyone to reach out to and felt lost and helpless. I knew I had to get out of it but didn't know how.

One day I was sitting with Mom and I asked her if she would like to read a poem my friend had written. She agreed and I showed her the poem he had written to me. After that, she pretty much figured out the rest of the story. 'It's a nice poem,' she said.

'We were together,' I said to her, 'but then we broke up.'

'When?' She asked.

'About two months ago.'

She wasn't angry with me, I sat there silently as all the

emotions rushed back and I wept bitterly. She held my hands and consoled me.

'Look, the only reason I didn't want you to get into a relationship was because I didn't want you to hurt yourself. I know that you've already gone through a lot in the past and relations at this age don't last too long. You will eventually find someone for yourself, but till then you must wait.'

Her reasons made complete sense to me. Once again she had understood me. I hugged her tight and cried away all the pain. I felt good after that. The pain didn't vanish but it definitely became bearable.

Priya Narayan

Two Options

I was thirteen when my parents got divorced and re-married. Our custody was granted to my father; I am not sure if he wanted my elder brother and me, but he got us, and so did his young wife.

My brother and I tried our best to adjust, but I guess it wasn't easy for our stepmother to suddenly become a mother to two grown–up children when she was only thirty-two.

I remember going to my father a few months after things started to get bitter between us. The man whom I had always loved and looked up to, had become a stranger to me in the past few months.

'Dad, can I speak to you about something?' I asked hesitantly.

'I hope this is not about some complaint from your school. You need to be studying hard.' Lately, he had become extremely critical of me.

'Dad, I want to stay in my school hostel. I have already spoken to my Principal and she is willing to make an exception for me even though we live in the same city. I can't study here, at home.' It had taken me two weeks to muster up the courage to talk to him.

As expected, he was furious. 'What will people say? I will become the laughing stock of the family. First it was your mother and now it's you — is this your mother's idea?'

'No! Dad, please! I think it will be better for your marriage too if I went away for a few years. Please think about it.'

I was aware that there was trouble brewing in his paradise because of us. My stepmother came from a less affluent family than ours. She was not used to certain luxuries that we took for granted. For instance, she believed in keeping the fridge in her bedroom, under lock and key, until she got back from work. She limited our access to other things as well and tried to keep me away from my father. I loved to snuggle up with him and sleep till late on Sundays. She pushed me aside as soon she became his wife.

I had to go to her every time I needed money as my allowance had been stopped. Once, when I asked her for money to buy sanitary towels, she showed me how to tear up an old bed sheet, stuff cotton in it and tie it around with elastic bands. 'Money doesn't grow on trees. We have to save up for your wedding,' she had reasoned.

She was a young woman and I was a rebellious teenager. She was also a little jealous and insecure when it came to my mother. When she wore my mother's jewellery, it made my blood boil. We argued often and my father had to mediate at such times. This must have taken a toll on their newly wedded bliss.

After a few days my father dropped a bomb on me. 'You are almost sixteen and old enough to get married. I have two options for you. First, you can continue to stay here, study hard and we will get you married when you turn eighteen. We will find you a family that allows you to continue your education. Second, you can move out now and go to the hostel, or to your mother, or to your mother's parents — wherever you like. I will pay three hundred rupees every month towards your expenses until you turn eighteen and then it will stop. If you take the second option, I do not want to see you ever again.'

I was shocked and speechless. My brother was very angry. 'How can you ask a sixteen-year-old to make such a big decision? And those options are terrible — she really has no choice. Why are you doing this?'

My father had made up his mind. 'If you feel so strongly about this, you should go as well.'

My brother stood up. 'We will take the second option. She and I will both leave so you can live in peace.'

I followed my brother to our room and we began to pack. Our stepmother came by to tell us that we had to leave the following day and that we should only take what belonged to us. We waited for our father to come and say goodbye to us the next morning. He didn't come but his wife came to check what we had packed. We opened our suitcases. I had taken an alarm clock that my father had given me and she looked at it suspiciously. I told her that I was taking it with me to mark the time I had spent in his house.

True to his word, my father ceased to be in our lives from that day. His three hundred rupees came until I turned eighteen and was barely enough to cover my expenses. My brother never got a penny from him. We survived and drew strength from one another. We lived on our own, finished our education, found jobs to support ourselves, got married and now have our own families.

Our teenage years, the best days of our lives were a mammoth struggle, but that only made us stronger. We learnt that nothing is impossible and that there will always be obstacles to test our mettle but the choice would always lie with us — either to find a way around them or to let them stop us. Those were the two options before us and we chose the first one!

Shaphali Jain

Understanding Love

Reluctantly, I get off the plane, missing New York already. I could not help but wonder for the umpteenth time why we had moved to Dubai. This was my eleventh move! At sixteen, all I wanted to do was hang out with friends and finish school. Apart from that, New York had been the only place I felt I belonged.

'Shanti beti,' Dad patted me on my shoulder. 'How was your flight?'

'Fine,' I said thinking about the irony of my name, which meant 'peace' and that was the emotion that had been lacking in my life.

Being an only child I was lonely and had no one to talk to. I resented my parents, specially my mother whom I blamed for everything that went wrong in my life.

'Taxi!' yelled Dad, though he didn't have to; this wasn't New York. There were over a dozen empty taxis waiting outside the airport as we stood there in the humidity.

We scrambled into one soon and fifteen minutes later I was standing in front of my new home — a tall high-rise building with glass windows that was located between the other high-rise buildings on the beach. I guess anyone coming from a country where winters are terribly cold would be happy to see a beach but I couldn't focus on anything but my misery.

'This is a very safe country,' said my Dad. 'They have the best of both worlds here — India and U.S.'

Yup — there are only two worlds in my dad's eyes.

I quietly walked into my room, taking in my new surroundings. There, in front of me, was a big poster of New York city. Tears welled up in my eyes.

'Do you like your room?'

I couldn't respond. My thoughts raced to New York — shopping, bowling with friends, going to school, watching movies and … just being happy.

'Shanti!' yelled Mom.

'What?' I screamed back, frustrated that she had brought me back into reality.

'This child will never learn,' Mom yelled again. 'Don't say "what", say "yes", and lower your voice when you talk.'

'Yes, Mom,' I replied sarcastically.

'Do you want something to eat?'

'No!' I yelled. 'I want nothing. Don't want to eat anything or go anywhere, I just want to be alone.'

'Beta,' said Dad ignoring the argument we were having, 'see, we got your favourite colour blanket and the dresser you wanted.'

'Thanks, Dad,' I gave him a weak smile. 'I'm a little tired right now so ….'

'Oh, here,' He handed me a small golden box, 'this is from your Maasi.'

I took it in my hands and sat down on my new queen-sized bed. I stared at the box wondering if she had actually left it for me. As if reading my mind, Dad said, 'She wanted to give it on your eighteenth birthday but since she is no more, I felt you should have it now.'

When I was growing up, Maasi had been my closest friend and a role model. I could talk to her about anything, even boys. I could be myself with her, very different from the relationship I had with Mom. But all that was in the past; I lost her and both my cousins in a car crash while they were driving to our house from Minesotta.

It had been Maasi's birthday and she was coming over for dinner. My mom had cooked all the things that she loved. I was very excited about meeting her but for some reason she was late. Suddenly the phone rang and I heard my mother scream. She had lost her sister, the only family she had left.

I was devastated. How I wished I had died with her. I was numb and furious at the drunken driver who had killed her and angry with my mother as well! I blamed her for Maasi's death. I often wondered if she felt any pain at all.

After her death I started getting into a lot of fights in school, so when we moved to New York, I was happy as I needed a fresh start ....

***

I'm not sure how long I slept, but it was dark outside when I woke up. I switched on my bedside lamp. My eyes fell on the box. Several thoughts rushed through my mind, as I opened the box with trepidation.

Inside the box was some jewellery, seashells and a couple of letters. I unfolded the first letter.

'My dear sweet Shantu ... '

I started to cry. Maasi was the only one who called me 'Shantu'. Taking a deep breath, I proceeded.

They say a Maasi is like a second mother. And you are very much like a daughter to me! Your mother will never tell you what I am about to, because she wants to protect you from pain. While your Nani worked long hours to put food on the table, your mother was the one who took care of us, packed our lunches, took us to school, and helped us with our homework. She even quit studies, so she could take care of us. She gave us everything in return for nothing.

When your Nani passed away, your mom had to be strong for us. Soon after, we lost our twenty-year-old brother to a rare disease. She took care of the funeral arrangements and put on a brave face only for me. What I am today is because of her sacrifices. She has been my strength and I know she will be yours too.

You are a lot like her; beautiful, courageous, strong, stubborn and protective. That's why I love you so much!

Remember every person in your life — good or bad — is a reflection of you, and every obstacle is an opportunity to grow and become a better person. You create your own destiny!

Your loving, Maasi.

I started crying. My mom rushed into the room.

'Shanti?' She looked worried. 'What's wrong?' She saw the letter in my hand and read it as she held me in her arms.

'Shantu,' my mom said and started crying too.

And as we wept together, I began to forgive — forgive my mom, myself.

My mom had let her guard down, something she hadn't done since my Nani passed away.

I had never known what she had gone through. Covering her sadness under a tough exterior, she had been a pillar of strength for her family. I had always seen a bitterness in her which I had never understood. If only she had shared everything with me, our life would have been so different!

In the background, we could hear the first Muslim prayer for the new day.

That day our relationship changed forever. It was a new beginning. Finally I felt at peace — 'Shanti'.

Ashima Suri

5

ON FAMILY AND LOVE

It is not flesh and blood but the heart which makes us fathers and sons.

–Johann Schiller

Cycle of Life

Going to school by bus had an advantage; you could say, 'Ma'am, the bus was late.' But there were a couple of disadvantages as well. First, your pocket money was going into the conductor's brown leather bag and second, the girls didn't look at you while you stood in the early morning assembly, because you didn't have a cycle.

My school was located right next to a college called Lady Doak College for Girls. We had shortened it to LDC, which for us stood for Love Developing Centre. The boys with their shiny cycles would stand near the bus stop and wait for the girls to ask, 'Has bus number 23B left?'

I know of three such boys who made it to the hall of fame with their cycles.

Boy 1: He swore that he glimpsed love in a girl's eyes when she asked him if the bus had left. He didn't actually find his true love that time, but he still stands at the same spot, only now with his Pulsar bike.

Boy 2: He would make plans to elope with one of the girls in LDC every day. He hasn't eloped yet though.

Boy 3: He almost married one of the girls in LDC. He fought with his parents over her and then with her rich father who sent goons to sort out the issue. That is when he stopped dreaming and started studying.

Growing up in these circumstances was tough. Every day, I was snubbed by the eight hundred-odd pretty girls just because I didn't have a cycle. All that I ever wanted from God was a red BSA SLR. The colour and the brand were decided after careful thought; girls love red (hint: red roses) and the low height of the BSA SLR would conceal my lack of height.

I asked my mother for the cycle six months before my birthday. After three months, she managed to break the news to my father. That is the time my father started saving for my cycle — it cost nine hundred rupees then.

On my birthday, it was raining hard. At 8 p.m. there was a knock on the door. It was my father with the cycle! We stayed seven kilometres outside the city and he had to cycle that distance in the heavy rain to bring home my new bicycle.

The teenager that I was, my first statement was, 'But this is an Atlas Goldline! I wanted a BSA SLR. I don't want this cycle.'

My father didn't say a word. He gave the cycle keys to my mother, changed into dry clothes, poured himself a peg of Old Monk rum and sat down in front of the TV.

Today, I shudder when I think of what must have gone through my father's mind at that moment, now that I know first-hand the love with which parents get gifts for their kids. My daughter has taught me the meaning of gratitude.

Last Saturday, we bought a blue and yellow cycle for Rhea. Unlike me, she is a grateful child and openly expressed her delight. She loves her cycle!

Jamshed Velayuda Rajan

Father, Brother and Finally Friend ...

I remember smiling awkwardly when my family talked about how my brother held me in his hands when I was born, and how he made me play cricket with him when I was hardly two or three. Even the photographs in the family albums seemed weird. My brother and I had an age difference of ten years, so we hadn't had time to connect much. It was as if there was an entire generation between us. He was almost like a second father to me.

***

I stood at the entrance of the airport gate and stared around in amazement. I was in the sixth grade and excited that my elder brother was leaving for further studies to the US. I was happy too, as now I could move into a room of my own and wouldn't have to shore with my parents anymore.

My brother smiled and bent down to touch everyone's feet while I simply stared. I pushed my way towards him after a few moments and looked up at him, smiling. He bent down and kissed my forehead, I smiled at him cheerfully and waved goodbye. He turned with a wink in my direction, and went inside. I thought I glimpsed a tear in his eye when he winked at me, but maybe it was just the bad lighting. We waited till his plane took off and then went home.

I would not say I missed him a lot. I had not realised his significance in my life then. Sure he missed me ... but I did not miss him untill he came for a short time and left again in December when I was in my ninth grade. That was the first time I cried at the airport when he was leaving. He was surprised at my emotion and hugged me tighter, perhaps understanding that I was finally starting to miss him. He came back again the next year in December when I was in my tenth grade, the board year, and spent time with me, advising me how to write my papers and cautioning me not to be too tense. He sounded more like a brother now.

After completing my board exams in March, I went to visit him in the US with my parents. My parents had to return after fifteen days due to the sudden death of my grandmother and I stayed on there with my brother. We managed somehow; he took care of my lunch and went to work, and in the evenings, he came back late and took me to some nice place for dinner.

That vacation proved to be the best bonding time for my brother and me. We took lots of photographs and I shared almost all my thoughts with him, keeping him awake till five in the morning, even if he had office to attend the next morning. Now he had become more like a friend and somehow, it felt better that way.

After all these years, I can now say that I look forward to meeting him more than just waiting for those chocolates which he invariably brought for me. I am still the irritating little sister he took care of and he's still an irritating brother who always talks about things that are beyond my understanding. Now, thanks to certain situations, we have come to realise the importance of our relationship. I eagerly wait for him to visit this December, hoping that our bond grows strong enough to make him stay here forever.

Manushi Desai

I'm Loving It

My sister tells me that on most days she feels as if she's a refrigerator since my niece keeps telling her, 'Mom, just chill.' Most mother across the world definitely dreads the teenage phase — mood swings, eating disorders, defiance, leave-me-alone ... the issues are many. But as an aunt, I' m loving this phase of my teenage niece (I hope, this article doesn't come to my sister's notice!).

My niece Sigma is the first-born child of our family and she's definitely pampered a lot. I have not spent much time with her during her growing up years as we lived in different cities and due to my job, I hardly got more than two weeks leave.

And now suddenly I see her as a teenager (on hindsight, it wasn't so sudden). Her closet is full of brands I recognise and love. Moisturisers, cleansers, lipsticks and eye-liners lie on the dressing table vying for her attention. And this time when I was home, I desperately tried getting into her twenty-eight size Levis jeans but had to leave it halfway when it just refused to move up. I was pretty disappointed. Looking at my face she said, 'Don't worry Maasi, this should motivate you to lose weight.' Before I could react, I saw her lying on the floor showing me the right way to do crunches. Yes, unlike her aunt, she's a fitness freak and like most teenagers, she's quite calorie-conscious and believes in eating healthy.

As my sister is at her wit's end dealing with a teeanage daughter, Google chat has become the link between me and my niece. It's always a pleasure to see a green dot against her name and her warm greetings peps up my mood instantly.

In October, 2010, I had my first holiday with her on a beach resort and we had a gala time just laughing and revelling in the dancing waves. Even as we entered our suite, we danced to 'Munni badnam hui' and forced my elder sister to record it on her handy cam for posterity. During this trip, I also saw a very caring travel partner in my teenage niece. On my way to the resort, when I expressed my desire to have those oily yet delicious (in my opinion) samosas from a roadside stall, she immediately asked the driver to stop, and soon I was gorging on 'potato-green pea' samosas.

She kept calling room service for delicious dishes like prawn pakodas, caramel custard and fruit salads. As I was still nursing a wrist injury, she was always there to open cans or bottles for me. On the beach, she rode a horse like a perfect 'Jhansi ki Rani' (she loves history). Both of us took a liking for a stray dog and we named him Bholu. As the morning sun played hide-and-seek with the waves, we bought food for Bholu and fed him. And sitting on the beach amidst rolling waves, she talked about her friends, teachers and their pranks in school. I talked about my friends, colleagues and work. Suddenly I realised that we could actually talk about quite a few things. On our way back, we listened to a song on her iPod. The joy of sharing music suddenly assumed a new meaning.

The holiday is now like a distant memory. I'm back at my workplace and she's back at her school preparing for her board exams. When I look at our holiday photographs, I feel a deep sense of camaraderie with her. I see a friend in her, and remember her words during the trip: 'Maasi, you must buy one of those cool Fast Track bags which have just hit the market.'

I followed her advice and hare just bought a cool blue and red bag. Now apart from a passion for music, food and films, we have one more thing in common — a sling bag and a warm relationship without any baggage to carry. The child for whom I had bought tiny pink colour frocks from Delhi's Sarojini market has grown up to be a beautiful teenager. Maybe, it's time for me to now buy her an LBD. And needless to say, I'm still desperate to get into her jeans!

Deepika

Lessons from My Grandpa

It was Christmas Eve and all of us had just finished dinner. I followed Grandpa as he went out to feed his dog Oscar. Grandpa loved pets and always had one, ever since I could remember. Grandpa had mixed some rice with butter and put the food in his bowl on a sheet of butter paper. I was always up to some pranks so I hid behind Grandpa and snatched the butter paper away while Oscar was eating. In a flash, he bit me.

There was a lot of commotion as everyone gathered around me. 'Call the doctor!' my grandma screamed in panic. I was scared and the pain was unbearable. Tears started rolling down my fat cheeks and I started howling at the top of my voice. After a while, when the fuss had died down and peace had been restored, Grandpa just quietly cleaned the wound with Dettol and put some ointment on it as the gash was not too deep.

After the incident, everyone thought I would shy away from dogs but even after being bitten by Oscar, I always tried to find a way to tease him by pulling his tail or some such thing. My tomfoolery never ceased.

Grandpa also had a chicken as a pet a while ago. He called her Pipip. Whenever he sat down to eat, Pipip would perch herself on his shoulder. My Grandpa would feed Pipip, and when she was really hungry, she would peck at his neck asking for more food. He would be very patient with all his pets and loved them immensely. It was easy to tell that Oscar also loved Grandpa a lot and would follow him all the time, wagging his tail.

Strangely I was jealous of the friendship they shared. I wanted Oscar to come and sit beside me. But of course, he never would. He wouldn't even play with me, and as for Pipip she flew away whenever I went close to her.

Disheartened I asked Grandpa how I could make them love me the way they loved him. He smiled and said, 'It's very simple, you just have to love them a lot and feed them when they are hungry.'

'So if I start feeding Oscar, will he come and stand near me as well?' I asked innocently.

'Maybe,' he replied.

So the very next evening, I took Oscar's supper to feed him. He was there, loyal as ever, sitting outside. When he saw me he backed off, so I just put the food in front of him, but he waited for me to go away before he started eating. I could sense he didn't trust me at all and it broke my heart.

I kept on trying but the situation never changed. Once after I gave him his food, I tried to pat his tail, but before I could touch him Grandpa grabbed me from behind and explained that he might bite if I disturbed him. Grandpa taught me a lot about animals — how important it is to be kind and gentle with them, to get them to trust you and many small things which had never seemed important to me before.

I could never make friends with Oscar as he never let me come near him. He didn't trust me till the day he died. Grandpa arranged for his funeral with a heavy heart and I could see his pain. He put a rose on the grave everyday — it was like a promise to remember all the good times they shared.

Oscar's death was the end of a lovely friendship between Grandpa and his beloved dog, but a new beginning for me. Grandpa gifted me a small puppy, whom I lovingly named Bloosi. This time I made sure I remembered all that Grandpa had taught me. I feel so happy and proud when Bloosi follows me around like Oscar had once followed Grandpa.

Banani Saikia

My Guardian Angel

Thud! The door slammed behind me. A wave of annoyance swept over me. I wanted to punch hard on the concrete walls of my room. I was walking in circles trying to slow down, relax my troubled mind and see reason. I wanted to open the door and scream at the man standing outside that door. The man on whose face I had just slammed the door again.

That man was my father, who loved me more than anything else and for whom I was the world. In my earliest memories, he has always held me closely and dearly, protecting me. He has never said a word or done anything that might hurt me. He has taken care of me and given me more love than any mother could have given her child. My mother had died giving birth to me.

I have never loved my father as much as he loved me. Especially now in my teenage, I have always revolted against him hurt his feelings. Sometimes I do it on purpose and though I know what I am doing is not right or fair, I really can't seem to help it.

As I stood in my room, the thoughts of my past rushed into my mind, and my eyes flooded with tears. Pictures flashed through my mind — his hand holding mine when I was lost and scared, reassuring me that he would be there for me no matter what, his tight and warm hug when I needed it the most, his guidance, his patience with me and how he made it to every single match I played, despite having a tight schedule.

Why does he have to love me so much, I thought. I'm not worth his love. I scream at him, I am angry at him, fight with him, hurt him and even when the fault is mine, he apologises, says sorry and patiently adjusts to my moods.

Today, he had asked me if I would have dinner with him as he was going to cook a new Italian dish he had learnt (I like Italian food). He had asked me if I could postpone my plans for another day and I picked a fight with him, was completely unreasonable and angry for nothing, as he stood dumbstruck, not understanding what had gone wrong.

I realised that I had been taking advantage of him and decided that it's all going to change. I decided that I was going to say sorry this time and put an end to my past behaviour. As I wiped my tears and braced myself to open the door and apologise, I heard a knock on the door.

'I'm sorry, son. We can have dinner together another day. I can cook anytime; you go ahead and spend time with your friends.'

I heard his footsteps walking away from my room. My heart pounded. I have to apologise now, I thought. I couldn't control my tears — I opened the door and rushed towards him, jumped on him with a tight hug and cried for a long time. He was startled at the way I was acting and so was I!

'I'm sorry, Dad. It's all my fault. I won't behave like this ever again, I will really try to change,' I said. 'I love you, Daddy,' I repeated through my tears.

He held me tight. 'I love you too, son! Now run along and have fun.'

'I'm not going anywhere and you are going to cook for me. Things will be different from now on. I love you, Daddy,' I said again, as I wiped tears off my face.

I couldn't stand there. I have never done anything like this before. I don't know why, but I ran back to my room after catching a quick glance of my father's smiling face. I felt I had told him something I had wanted to say for a long time. I heard his soft 'I love you too, son' before I closed the door.

Kamalesh Babu J.

My Mother's Daughter

My mother separated from my dad when I was thirteen and moved to Hyderabad, her home town. It was decided that my siblings and I would stay on with Dad in Bangalore. In the pre-internet days of the late Eighties, we spoke to her occasionally on the phone and met her mostly during holidays. However her deep influence on my angst-ridden, troubled teenage life was tremendous.

We had often been at loggerheads. I was the spoilt, first grandchild of the family and it was her first time as a mother. We clashed often and I have vivid memories of her yelling at me to pick up my clothes from the floor, insisting I have a bath at the most crucial moment during *Star Trek* and frightening me by insisting she was going to marry me off as early as possible!

What I also remember is how I would lie down on her bed after a long day at school and tell her the smallest details of my day. What my friends said, which boy was cute, which teacher knew nothing — my opinion on anything and everything under the sun. She always had the time to listen to me. She would lie down next to me, listen with great interest, and enjoy hearing about my day, as much as I would enjoy sharing it with her.

Mum lived life on her own terms and broke many norms because she felt it was more important to find happiness, than to care about what people felt. To do this, she had to take the path less travelled of doing what is right and not what is easy or favoured by society. She re-married, had another child, and admirably juggled her duties as a mother and wife, so that none of us felt neglected. She showed us that a life lead with dignity and self-respect works out in the end and is worth the struggle.

She was also very liberal. She let us wear what we wanted, spoke the language of the young — a few words were off limits, but due to her own colourful vocabulary, she wasn't so rigid about us using slang and the occasional cuss word. She brought us up to respect all faiths, castes, creed and colours. She loved to travel, eat out, go to the movies, shop and was always (and still is) up for a bit of fun.

There were some things though, that were not negotiable. Faith in God and his love, praying, keeping the faith, and trying to be the best person one could be, was what she expected of us. And we had no choice but to follow.

This held us in good stead even when we were apart and I needed a gentle hand to guide and steer me safely through my teenage years. When in doubt, I would ask myself what my mother would want me to do. So, rather regretfully, I stayed clear of boyfriends, smoking, drinking and the unmentionable — sex (which incidentally my mother spoke to me at length many times). In hindsight I am glad I followed her voice in my head.

It's difficult to have your parents breakup. It's possible though, to turn out fine and be a happy, secure person. The secret to our success stems from the fact that my mother never expected otherwise. She believed we were stars and would always shine, come what may.

When I turned eighteen and took driving lessons, she was thrilled and waited impatiently for me to start driving. However it took me a full year to muster enough courage to take the car out on my own. I will never forget how shocked Mum was at my seeming inability to master this new skill. 'I know you can do it,' she reassured me repeatedly. 'You just have to try!' One day, I just got into the car and began to drive. I love driving now and am thrilled when people tell me I drive well. The credit, though, goes to my Mum and her unwavering belief in my ability to do just about anything.

I have a little girl now, and though I find it hard to put aside all the other stuff I love to do — chat on the phone, check Facebook, update my blog — I think back on those golden moments Mum and I spent together, and I sit down to talk to my little darling and try to be a part of her world while I still can.

Mum called me the other day (she had heard me admonishing my daughter whilst I was on the phone with her), and in her gentle, loving way, advised me on how essential it is to make time for our children and hear them out. 'It's good for their confidence and builds self-esteem,' she said.

I know, Mum. I know.

Zainab Sulaiman

Of Love and a Necklace

'It's already six! And you are not up yet! God knows what is wrong with you! Look at your friends ... they must be studying by now! And you! Get up quickly now!' Well, that fine morning began with these words from Mom. Actually every morning begins with the same words; I don't even expect any change in her style of waking me up. I mean, it hasn't changed for the past I-don't-know-how-many years and it's of no use expecting it to change now. Poor me, I have accepted it as the wake-up tune of my alarm clock! I woke up and rubbed my eyes sleepily. Mom continued her how-to-be-a-good-girl sermon. She went on, and on and on ... oh! I was getting irritated now, and I chose to go to my grandparents' home. They happen to be my immediate neighbours and they pamper me a lot.

Just then, the telephone rang and my aunt proceeded to answer it. 'Hello! Oh, hi! Is that true? Great! That's a wonderful piece of news! So which date have you decided on?' And after a small pause, she continued, 'We will surely be present there. Congratulations to you!' As expected, she excitedly told us that my uncle would be getting married next month. I jumped in delight! He was one of my favourite uncles, and I was really close to him. It was after all a golden opportunity for me to meet all my family members and most importantly, dress up beautifully and flaunt all my lehengas and other exquisite dresses in my wardrobe. The thought made me smile widely. My aunt invited me to go shopping with her and I readily agreed. Shopping is one of my favourite pastimes, even if it is buying grocery or vegetables or spices for the kitchen.

We left a few hours later and decided to visit the central market. As my aunt busied herself selecting a wide variety of skin and face-care products, I preferred to have a look at the jewellery on display. A beautiful necklace of white stones, with a unique design caught my attention. My eyes were glued on it. I asked the shopkeeper to show it to me. He smiled and opened the box for me to see. It sparkled in the light and was absolutely gorgeous. I wanted to buy it and wear it to the wedding. My aunt noticed me with the necklace and asked me if I liked it. I nodded. Immediately she asked the shopkeeper the price. He said, 'Rs 1649, Madam. Now I knew I could not buy it. I just kept quiet and went out of the shop quietly. But I kept thinking of the necklace. I wanted to save money and buy it, but saving that much would take me quite a lot of time and my uncle's wedding celebrations would end by then.

As soon as I arrived home, I raced to my room, closed the door with a loud thud and heard a subsequent 'Are you planning to break that door?' from Mom. I knew I should apologise, but that could wait a bit, I thought. I opened my cupboard, took out my wallet and began to count the money I had saved (including the 50p and Re 1 coins). I realised that my savings amounted to a meagre sum of Rs 219.50.

Goodness! What was I going to do? I would not be able to buy that necklace. Quietly and sadly, I went to my mom, said sorry to her, and retreated to my room.

In the evening, I went to spend some time with my grandma, who usually has a solution to all my problems. Her sweet smile has the power to make me forget all my worries. I entered her room and sat down beside her. She asked me, 'You liked the necklace a lot, didn't you?' I was astounded. It must have been my aunt who told her, as no one else knew about the necklace. She said that an aunt who resided in the US and another aunt, who stayed in Ahmedabad, had just called her and requested her to buy me the necklace, saying that they would pay her when they visited their hometown, Bhubaneswar.

Just then, my mom too appeared and told me that she would like to gift it to me. My aunt too gave me the money and told me to buy the necklace. I had always considered her to be a big miser, as she seldom gave me anything, except love, advice and her funny jokes. I was thrilled, firstly, at the idea of getting the necklace, but secondly, and most importantly, I was touched by the gesture of all my family members. Like a normal teen, I was getting closer to my peer group. But that day, I realised I have such warm people who love me, care for me and understand me.

I bought the necklace the very next day and wore it to the wedding. Everyone said that the necklace shimmered and sparkled in the light. Deep in my heart, I knew that it shone with my family's love for me. It was exquisite and special to me, just like my family.

Sigma Samhita

Sisterhood

My sister and I had an age gap of several years between us, and we weren't exactly close to each other. I mean, we had been fairly close till childhood; she had always been the big sister I looked up to and idolised. Whatever she and her boarding school friends did, became a cool thing for me. But as we grew up, we gradually drifted apart.

She had enrolled into one of the most prestigious boarding schools of Dehradun at the age of twelve. Naturally, when I reached the same age, everyone in the family expected me to follow her example. But I didn't. I couldn't. I had only just found a niche for myself in high school (and everyone knows how difficult that is — finding your own niche during the awkward pre-teen years). It wasn't just any place (in the shaky social hierarchy of school) but a place at the very top! I didn't want to give up on all that and go through the entire ordeal of adjusting to a new environment all over again. If my sister was disappointed, she did not show it.

Besides, my world was swiftly changing. Suddenly, the loose football shorts I had practically lived in all my childhood, were replaced with trendier short skirts. The tomboy caps we once wore askew, were discarded for funkier hair extensions.

My sister and I couldn't have been more different from one another. If I liked pink, she liked black. If I listened to Britney Spears, she listened to Aerosmith. She was the more 'organising a protest march' type. I was more for cutting out heart-shaped cookies and conducting bake-sales. Naturally, differences arose and we no longer had anything in common. Whenever she came home for her break, we were both very silent and awkward around each other.

On one such occasion, she had come home for the Diwali-Dusshera break. It being the festive season, the entire family was in a celebratory mood and everyone was busy with the preparations. I, too, was very excited and had got a heavily embroidered lehenga stitched especially for the occasion.

That Diwali had been an evening of festivities and celebration, but sadly, it was also the evening of my first heartbreak. Sad and dejected, I did not join my family for the celebrations at our neighbour's place. Instead I chose to sit and sulk on the doorstep, burying my head in my arms.

It was then that my sister entered through the gates, dressed all in black (no, she wasn't celebrating. The radical environmentalist in her did not allow her to celebrate an occasion that brought about so much noise and air pollution). When she noticed me so forlorn, sitting on the doorstep, my lehenga spread around me, and my head buried in my arms, she climbed up the front steps and squatted down beside me in her checked shorts and grey sneakers, asking me what the matter was.

Hurt and miserable as I was, somehow at that time, looking into her calm, sure eyes, the entire story came tumbling out. She listened patiently, as I poured out all my troubles to her. When I was done, she nodded simply and handed me some water, and left me there to go about her business. I stared after her, chiding myself to have expected any sort of comforting from someone I barely knew any more.

Suddenly I heard howls of pain that came from somewhere in the vicinity and the howls were shortly followed by my sister dragging by the collar, the (now terrified) jerk who had upset me in the first place. She made him apologise. Apparently, she had punched him in the face (there was something trickling down his nose), before giving him a piece of her mind. I didn't know whether to laugh hysterically or to panic at the trouble she had got us into. And even though it was I who ended up apologising to him for the broken nose (she felt it unnecessary), it was altogether a memorable incident.

Later, we sat together on the doorstep — she in her black T-shirt and checked shorts, and I in the heavy silk lehenga and gauzy dupatta — talking about each other's lives and making up for all the lost time.

And that is how I ended up spending my Diwali — sitting on the doorstep under the brilliant sky, playing cards with my sister and sipping Pepsi (for her, healthy orange juice), laughing and fondly remembering the old times. I look back and smile at the thought of how I lost my sister a few years back, only to find her again several years later, amidst a flurry of playing cards, mouthfuls of gujjia, a broken nose and a spectacular overhead display of sparkling stars, on a seemingly ordinary Diwali eve.

Harshita Bartwal

Thicker Than Blood

I stormed out of the house banging the door behind me as tears rolled down my cheeks. I wiped them away with the back of my hand but they just wouldn't stop.

I felt betrayed. How could she do this to me? After all the things we had done together and all the wonderful times we had shared. How could she keep the truth from me and lie to me all this time? As much as I didn't want to believe it, now I knew it was the truth and I hated her for it. For so many years she had kept my identity from me. How could I be expected to forgive her? I no longer knew who I was.

I had loved her from the bottom of my heart and her simple confession had shattered me beyond words. I felt numb as I sat on the rocks in the deserted beach with the breeze on my face. The times I had spent with her flashed across my mind like a movie, how she had fed me, taught me cycling, made me laugh when I was mad at her, held my hand when I had fever, wiped my tears when I got into fights at school, how we laughed and the times we cried together. The spate of tears refused to ebb.

Suddenly as the scenes replayed in my mind over and over again, a sudden realisation dawned and with it emerged a feeling of calmness and joy.

How could I hate someone who had given me a new life? One that had more than I could ask for. She had done nothing wrong! Nothing wrong at all! As a matter of fact, she had taken me from an orphanage where my real mother had left me, for whatever her reasons might have been. She had given me a beautiful beginning and because of her I had loving parents and a home. If there was any anger, it ought to be towards the person who left me.

So what if she didn't give birth to me? She was my mother in every way and how she loved me! She needed me now and here I was being so selfish. I wiped my tear-stained cheeks and ran back to the house.

I opened the door and stepped inside the house. I saw her, staring out of the window, sobbing. My heart ached on seeing her red, puffy eyes. 'Mom,' I whispered, trying to hold back tears.

She stood up and walked unsteadily towards me. Her hands cupped my face as she stammered in between sobs, 'I ... I - I'm sorry, Destiny ... please forgive me ... I-I love…' I didn't let her finish and went and hugged her. 'I love you too, Mom.'

We both broke down and wept uncontrollably. One thing I was now sure of, she may not have been my biological mother but our bond was thicker than blood.

As told to Akshika Agarwal

6

ACTS OF KINDNESS

If you want others to be happy, practice compassion. If you want to be happy, practice compassion.

–Dalai Lama

A Friend Found

Ragging someone and being a bully has never appealed to me. New students are as it is scared and insecure, and on top of that tormenting them doesn't seem like such a great idea. But to my utter dislike, my friend Archana enjoyed it more than anything. The moment she got to know that a new kid had settled in her dormitory, she would be itching to harass the poor kid.

Karishma, the new student in our class had just arrived. She was short and fair; her plaited hair hung untidily till her waist, and her skirt covered her knees. She had a grating voice and every time she spoke, it hurt the ears. It wasn't very easy to sympathise with her when Archana tyrannised her.

She was made to do all of Archana's laundry, her homework, make her bed, wake her up for morning PE class. If she didn't do any of these she was made to go through hell. Sometimes, I too gave her my math and physics homework, which I must say she did very efficiently. One thing to her credit was that she took all that we meted out with a sporting attitude. She probably thought sooner or later it would stop.

One night after the lights were off, Karishma was made to steal Maggi from the tuck room. We were in the middle of gobbling it down when the House Matron walked into our dormitory. We were caught red-handed. The entire incident was narrated to the Principal the next day. Archana, being the Vice House Captain, had an upper hand; she blamed the entire affair on Karishma.

Karishma was punished severely. She had to get up earlier than the entire hostel and do rounds on the field. Her coupons were confiscated for two weeks. Somehow I felt uneasy about the whole affair; I didn't want to betray my friends but my conscience would not let me forget this incident. I wrote an anonymous note to the House Matron, mentioning that Karishma was innocent and she was actually a victim of ragging.

Karishma was released from the torture though the involvement of 'others' was never found. I was glad to see her smiling again. From that day onwards, I did not let anyone push her around and decided I would not be party to any more bullying. Eventually she settled down and did very well in academics.

After the Tenth Standard, I went back to Delhi to be with my parents. To my surprise, Karishma and I were in the same school there in the Eleventh. She had taken up Science and I had chosen Commerce. I was amazed to see how soon she made a place for herself in a new school while I was still at sixes and sevens.

Soon she was elected Head Girl and the day the swearing ceremony took place, I couldn't help but think of the earlier times in the hostel. The moments we had terrorised her were still fresh in my memory. For a moment I thought she would make life hell for me; instead after the ceremony she came and gave me a big hug. Saving her from the unjust punishment earlier had found me a friend now. Yes, she had somehow guessed that it was me who had written that letter.

That day I learnt no one can take away your success and your future. If you have your goals set clear in your mind, even the biggest bullies cannot make you a loser. In spite of all that she had faced, she achieved success — a lesson that left a deep mark in my life. There will be phases in life when the world may seem like a dark tunnel but your determination can bring light and you can win over any obstacle.

We remain friends even today and hopefully for ever....

Arti Sonthalia

Monopoly Can Wait

It was our summer vacation, and while all other children were playing, my younger brother and I were busy looking for ways to earn some money.

Dhyan and I stood at the door of our neighbour's house on a blazing afternoon. We rang the bell and Mrs Shah opened the door. 'Mrs Shah, can we run an errand for you?' I requested. She looked surprised as I explained, 'We want to make some money by doing small jobs like watering the plants and washing the car.'

'Okay, I will give you twenty rupees for washing the car,' she said.

Why did we need the money? Well, my brother and I wished to buy Monopoly, the board game. My parents gave us one hundred rupees and two hundred rupees came in as birthday gifts from our grandparents. But we were still a hundred rupees short. Doing odd jobs for our wonderful neighbours seemed to be the perfect solution.

By evening we had completed our chores and had the hundred bucks we needed. Our yearning to buy the game was finally going to be satisfied. My younger brother was all smiles and giggles and I too was elated. We danced and yelled 'Monopoly! We have our Monopoly!'

At last we had the game. We stood at the shop holding it tight. The smell of the brand new game was a treat to our senses. After lunch, we decided to sit down to play and were about to begin when the doorbell rang. My mother went to answer it.

There was a man at the door. He introduced himself as a volunteer for an orphanage and asked if we would like to donate some of our old toys and clothes.

I was excited to start the game but suddenly I found my thoughts drifting in a different direction. I was thinking of the orphans. They had nobody to care for them and love them. Where were their parents? They did not have a mother's lap to sleep on and no father's finger to hold. I realised my life would be a total misery without my parents. It would be all black and white without the colours of fun and love. My eyes moistened.

I decided to do something for the orphans. Why not share our new game with them? I talked to my mother and brother. They readily agreed and we wrote a note to our new friends.

It read:

Hi Friends,

We are your new friends, Parth and Dhyan. We wanted to share this cool gift with you all. So, go ahead and enjoy it! Love you all!

Parth and Dhyan

It felt wonderful, and I realised that the joy of giving surpasses the joy of receiving!

Parth Patel

Pass It On ...

'Which is the way to the railway station? Is there a big Coop or Migros store over there?' I asked yet another lady who excused herself and walked away.

We were vacationing in Europe. I was strolling alongside Lake Lucerne with Mom and Dad. I wanted to go to either Coop or Migros, shops that stocked really good and comparatively cheaper local chocolates. One of the two stores was supposed to be near the Lucerne railway station and so we were asking passersby how to get to the place.

A couple of people pointed vaguely in the direction of the railway station. Then we came across two cheerful girls in their late teens. 'One last try,' I thought to myself and asked them if they knew any one of the stores I was looking for, and whether it was located nearby. They confirmed that both the stores were indeed located within walking distance. Then what they said next was most welcome, but totally unexpected. 'Shall we take you there?' they asked.

To say we were surprised is putting it mildly. Definitely, we had heard of people going out of their way to help others, but so far we hadn't had any such luck.

They accompanied us right up to the store, though we kept on saying repeatedly that we could find it on our own. They even asked if they could help in locating anything that we needed in particular inside the store.

I don't know whether they walked with us to just to show us the way or because they had to go there in any case. But because of their thoughtful gesture, whenever I remember my trip, I recall those two giggly teenagers, I look at the picture I took with them, which is now the background on my cell phone. It is a constant reminder of how nice it feels to be helped in a foreign country when we least expect it.

I used to offer to help people sometimes at my convenience. After this trip, however, I have made up my mind to help others every time I get a chance, even if it means going out of my way. My reply in response to the 'thanks' anyone might say, is only these three words: 'Pass it on.'

Soma Karnavat

Rendezvous with a Cuddly Bear!

The first thing that came to my mind was the word 'owl'. An oversized snow owl ogling at me over the rim of his glasses!

My classmate Anchal had set me up on a blind date with this unimaginable piece of human artwork! I frowned and kicked myself for agreeing. Forcing a smile, I wished that the arms of the clock would move faster.

During the course of our conversation, I realised that this 'owl' could turn into a hyena at times as he let out a queer laughter every now and then.

To break the ice we started discussing each other's favourite movies. He proudly announced that his was *Sholay* and broke into famous dialogues from the film. *Arre Oh Sambha … kitne admi the?* I felt nauseous as he next moved on to the Mausiji and Basanti scene.

Help!! I was terribly embarrassed and looked around to see if anybody was watching us. I noticed something strange going on at our neighbouring table. The guy was suddenly yelling at the girl sitting opposite him. 'Don't ever try to get in touch with me again. I'm through with girls like you!'

There was silence in the coffee shop except for the whimpering sounds from the poor girl who had just been humiliated publicly. Everybody looked at her with sympathy but no one wanted to interfere.

Suddenly, the 'owl' jumped up and in no time was standing besides the girl. 'Coward! Don't you have any shame, disgracing a girl in public?' The guy was taken aback and before he could retort, everybody else started jeering and booing him. The 'owl' then escorted the sobbing girl to our table and offered her a glass of water. I stared at him in disbelief.

The look in his eyes was gentle and he radiated confidence and compassion. What surprised me was that he was a radically different person after that, almost as if he had been putting up a façade of being weird all this while. It was amazing! The girl calmed down after some time and the three of us actually had a good time over coffee and sandwiches, as I discovered a potential good friend in him.

That is when I struck off the word 'owl' from my mental diary and replaced it with 'bear'. A cuddly lovable bear!

Priyanka Kadam

Thank You, Ma'am!

Throughout the years at college I have met different kinds of people. People I have liked, disliked, cherished and detested. But very few fell in the category of people I genuinely respected. One such person was Ms Lalitha Suhasini.

The first year of college was drawing to an end. Exams were round the corner. Attendance lists were put up on the notice boards, based on which admit cards for the first year university exams were to be given. And my attendance was short because while everyone was attending classes, I was either off campus for some competition or, generally, because I didn't quite like the class. The fact that I was constantly at loggerheads with my Principal didn't really make things any easier for me. He seemed rather decided on the fact that he wouldn't let me sit for my exams. It was a stalemate.

While most students in my class were preparing for the examinations with gusto and fear, I was way too preoccupied with peripheral issues. To make matters worse, tact wasn't really one of my virtues and that made it difficult for me to plead with the Principal, though in my heart I knew that losing out on a year would make a lot of difference to my parents, if not me.

Time flew by, and soon I realised that there was just a week to go before the examination. Two students had already been given their transfer certificates after having been informed that they would not get their admission cards. Theoretically, I could still make it if any of the lecturers vouched for the fact that I had missed the classes for study-related reasons. However, considering that I was up against the highest authority in the college, convincing any of the teachers to do that was unlikely. I tried, though.

Despite the fact that I tried to look as composed as possible, if truth be told, I was really worked up. I couldn't see any way out of it. The worry was gnawing away my insides. Some of my close friends who were in better positions did try to console me, but that was all that they could do. At the end of the day, they couldn't make up for my attendance.

Then one day, my English teacher, Ms Lalitha Suhasini called me to the staff room. My bonding with all the teachers in the English department was rather good, partly because I loved the subject and partly because they liked me since I was winning a lot of competitions for the college. When I walked in, the entire department was there. Lalitha Ma'am had always been a person I had genuinely respected because of her clear judgment of right and wrong and because she was one of those teachers who believed in me.

She offered me a deal. We had to take up language classes for the first two years and in the third year, we had just the core subjects. The deal was that she would give me attendance for all of her classes, irrespective of me having attended it or not but in return, I should show the Principal a little more respect and ensure that my attendance never slips below the required percentage for the following two years. The first part of the deal was tough but she told me that irrespective of how I feel about the Principal, the fact was that he was my guru and he deserved some respect for it. And I liked the way she explained it to me. I agreed.

To be very honest, it came as a major surprise because I never thought someone would stick their neck out this much for me. She stood the risk of losing her job. But she did it. My attendance went up and I just scraped through with an added fine of five hundred rupees.

Finally, I got a call from the Principal the evening before the first paper, and later that night, I received my admit card. I could tell from his expression that he hated the fact that he had to give me the ticket for the next academic year, and frankly, I quite liked the feeling.

To show my gratitude to Lalitha Ma'am, I scored above ninety per cent in her paper and a first class overall because I knew that nothing pleased her better than seeing her students succeed.

Since then, seven years have passed. Lalitha Ma'am is now married and settled in the US. It's been very long time since I spoke to her, though I do manage to catch her online once in a while. All said and done, I think she was one of the people who helped me shape up and gave me a clearer perspective on many things in life. I can only say, 'Thank you, Ma'am!'

Soumyarka Gupta

This is Tolerance!

I was abroad in a country called Timor Leste (East Timor) where my mother was on a United Nations mission. East Timor had just got its independence from Indonesia a few years back and was still relatively underdeveloped. It was difficult for me to adjust to life there.

My younger brother, my father, and I had joined my mother on 15 April, 2009. I was thirteen at that time. The family's plan was that my grandparents would join us in a couple of months, when my father would leave for India.

My grandfather had a tough time deciding whether or not to leave India and join us. He was seventy-two, and very different from any old man his age. He was a historian, who had written more than thirty books. He had exceptional self discipline and self-restraint.

He used to say, 'Time is the most important thing in our life. We should never waste our precious time on silly issues. Silliness is also a part of life, but only to some extent.'

He would not waste time like others by just sleeping and watching TV. He was very serious about his career of writing history books. He could walk fast like a young man and was able to do push-ups too! Moreover, he was incredibly tolerant and adaptable and when he arrived at Timor, he was not at all uncomfortable. Even in this alien land, with unknown people, he was as comfortable as in his own house in India.

My grandmother was a sweet old lady. She was like any other sixty-five-year-old woman. She was a somewhat 'over-caring' grandma; she used to take care of us so much that it got unbearable sometimes. Anyway, when they arrived in Timor, I was overjoyed.

We had to stay there for almost a year, but I couldn't go to school to attend my classes there. My mother requested my grandfather to be my teacher and help me in my studies. I had brought my books with me in order to keep up with the curriculum of my school in India. My grandfather started teaching me a just a couple of days after their arrival.

His routine was to sit with his laptop from early morning and write his books. Every day I got up around nine, which he disliked and instructed me to wake up early. I kept quiet for some months. I did not like to stay with such a serious man, living such a serious life. Though he was not always that annoying; he used to play football with us, watch movies, joke and help me catch some of those small cute mice which were always destroying things in my room. However, it was awful when he used to force me to study.

One day, when I was writing a story on his laptop, which he used to give me whenever he was free, I did something really wicked. I do not know what came over me; I deleted everything, all his hard work, everything he had written in those last four months. I thought it was a good way to take revenge. After that, I shut down the laptop and went off to sleep. Nevertheless, the next day, the incident haunted me. In the evening, while playing soccer, mother joined me instead of grandfather. When the game was over, and it was time to go home, mother took me to a quiet place, and asked me, 'Why did you delete everything from the laptop?'

I was stunned and speechless. I replied slowly after some time. My mother did not show any anger but told me that the previous night, when my grandfather had discovered my terrible act, he had sat with my mother outside, and had started crying while narrating what I had done. 'He sobbed,' she said. I was heartbroken.

The man who was so disciplined in his life, made best use of his time, and who, at seventy-two, had come all the way leaving his country just to take care of us, was thanked in this way. Is this what he deserved?

The amazing thing about this incident was that my grandfather did not say a single word to me about the damage I had done. He continued to help me in my studies in the same way he had done before, played with me too, but never discussed that incident with me.

His hard work, created painstakingly over months was erased but his tolerance was incomparable. Even today, when I think of what I did to him, I feel so guilty. How I wish I could be like him!

Anhad Mishra

7

EYE OPENERS

*W*do not see things as they are. We see them
as we are.

—Talmud

A New Direction

We had thought it would be one of those boring seminars on moral education. We had planned not to attend school that day. It would be better to stay at home and prepare for the exams beginning next week, I had thought. But what made me go to school that day, I still do not know.

The NGO that was holding the seminar grabbed our attention right from the start. Gender bias, rights of the girl child, battered women — all these issues were being discussed. It helped open our minds to the society beyond the cloistered walls of our school. My blood boiled as I realised with dismay that such conditions prevailed even now. Maybe in the villages such things happened, I thought, thinking of all the families I knew with daughters who were pampered as I was at home.

It was the last interactive session in the seminar, when we girls had been invited to ask questions, if any.

'Ma'am, my mother and I do so much work at home. My father comes home drunk every night and does not even sit with us. He does not beat or even shout at us, but he also does nothing which all my friends seem to enjoy doing with their dads. Do I have any right to demand this of my father? How do I make my mother happy?'

There was stunned silence in the auditorium. No one could imagine such a thing being uttered by a girl studying in one of the elite schools in the city. And certainly not by a girl who was otherwise silent in class, had just one or two friends, got poor grades and hardly took part in any class activities. Now all of us understood the reasons behind it.

Shweta then went on to relate how she had to cope with all the housework and look after her kid sisters before she could sit down to study. And her mother had to continuously work overtime, as money was never enough. Though it was not strictly an issue related to gender bias, it was a consequence of age-old societal restrictions on women. Such issues were never discussed openly and therefore the women in the family stoically bore all that happened to them.

The seminar had been aimed at instilling in us awareness about our rights as a girl child vis-à-vis the conditions prevailing in our society. And it had succeeded in its aim — all of us walked out that day, aware how deep-rooted the issue was. It was not something which happened to other people. It had happened to someone in our midst.

I picked up one of the pamphlets that the NGO volunteers had given us. I carefully put it away between the pages of my history book. It had given me a new direction in life. I was determined that one day I would do something for the cause. Until then, it would serve as a reminder that we have to understand each other if we are to solve such problems.

Sadhika Pant

A Teeny Affair

What attracted me at first was his full-throated laugh. His face was lit up with a brilliant smile, as he looked straight into my eyes from the far end of the pandal. Durga Puja celebrations were on, and in the background of the reverberating dhak and the heady incense of the dhuni, our eyes met.

He was with his friends and I was with mine. While I listened half-heartedly to what my friend was saying, my eyes followed him in the crowd. Festivities of the occasion instilled gaiety in our hearts, but the two of us were in a world of our own. So that was my first meeting with him, when he casually walked up to me and asked me my name.

I was in my teens and was just beginning to be aware of my own individuality. I found a friend in him, more than anything else. A man who was searching for a footing in the world for himself, moulded me according to his vision of the perfect woman. Was it strange that my ideas were coloured by his perspective? Yet, he left space around me to spread my wings and take flight to wherever my fancies took me.

At the most important juncture of my life, when I had to make a choice among various career options, he left me to make my own decision. From childhood I had wanted to study medicine. But now, all of a sudden, I was having misgivings. I wanted to leave aside science and found a growing interest in literature, psychology and philosophy.

I still vividly remember that day — I had gone to meet him right after my Biology practicals (in those days, dissection of chloroformed animals was part of the curriculum). I told him that I could not stand the sight of blood.

'Do you think I have it in me to study medicine? Should I sit for the medical entrance?' I asked him.

'You decide, after all it's a decision you will have to live with all your life,' was his noncommittal answer.

'Why don't you help me to decide?'

'How can I?'

I was miffed. I dropped the matter.

He did not give any advice or suggestions, just watched from a distance … and only when I had filled the forms for college after having decided to study literature, did he voice his opinion.

'I knew that you were not cut out to be a doctor,' he said.

'Why did you not say this earlier? It would have saved me a lot of sleepless nights and weighing the pros and cons,' I retorted.

'Remember, in the most important decisions of your life, do not depend on others. If I had said something, you would have been swayed into believing what I believed. And perhaps never known what you really wanted to do.'

From a teenage romance to a mature relationship, he never tried to influence me into seeing things his way, thereby making me self-dependent and confident. He knew that being a fiercely individualistic person, I would never be happy if I did not choose on my own. He has always been there for me, lest I stumble … never as a crutch, but as a step in the ladder I had to climb.

Kahlil Gibran has said, 'Let there be spaces in your togetherness.' My teenage friend, lover and now my husband for twenty three years, has made me realise just that.

Monika Pant

Awakening

As a teenager, I always had a complex about my average looks. Studying in a co-educational college and not having a boyfriend at the age of nineteen only made it worse. Despite being a brilliant student things did not change. The only thing that had changed was my parent's expectations, which were rising by the day.

Sudha was my best friend. Sometimes I felt she knew me better than I knew myself. She often reprimanded me for listening to the after-dinner nonsense in the hostel. I tended to get easily carried away while Sudha was more stable. In our sister-like relationship, she was undoubtedly the wiser one.

Sudha told me about Aakash, the boy from the science section who had been enquiring about me. Science didn't sound very interesting to me but before I knew, Aakash had asked me out for coffee. I hesitated but Sudha intervened and accepted the invitation on my behalf. I kicked her legs under the table. After he left, we stared at each other for a moment and then broke into giggles. We ran back to the hostel. The excitement was dawning on me. After trying out all the outfits, it was finally decided that I would wear an aqua blue Hilfiger T-shirt with white capris. It was my first date!

Coffee with Aakash was far more exciting than I had imagined. We couldn't stop talking. He knew exactly how to treat a girl. We fixed up our next date, which would be a drive in his new red Volkswagen. Aakash perfectly fitted the picture of the man of my dreams and my mind had already started wandering and making plans.

I couldn't stop beaming when I got back to the hostel. Sudha had been waiting anxiously. She wanted to know every detail and I obliged her willingly. The next few days drifted by with romantic thoughts of Aakash. We talked and texted all day and night. I longed to meet him. Sudha was happy for me but warned me to slow down.

We finally met again. He took me to a fancy Chinese restaurant for lunch, where we sat in a cozy corner. After lunch, we went to his fancy studio apartment. I had butterflies in my stomach. We were sitting on his lovely suede sofa when he kissed me. Initially, I was shy but soon I found myself giving in to all that he asked for. I had no control over myself, and felt intoxicated in his arms. It was all so perfect. I had wanted this and now when I had it, I suddenly felt uneasy. I asked him to stop. Aakash moved away looking disappointed. It was all happening too fast and I told him I needed time. He tried to convince me but I wanted to get back to the hostel. We drove back in silence.

I sat on my bed wondering if I had been foolish. Every girl was probably indulging in this so why did I run away? It was cool to have a boyfriend, make out with him and rave about it to your friends. What was it that had stopped me?

Sudha came over and I narrated what had happened. I told her that my conscience did not allow me to go further. My parents had sent me all the way to study and placed their trust in me. How could I let them down? That day I realised life was full of temptations and it is for us to know what to choose.

That night I prayed silently and thanked the Almighty for bringing me to my senses on time. I had to respect the freedom which my parents had given me.

This incident brought an awakening in me which guided me for the rest of my life. As for Aakash, Sudha told me that if he truly cared for me, he would call. He never did and I was glad.

I was a wiser person and that year I topped the university.

Arti Sonthalia

Beautiful

'Roll no. 37', shouted Ms Sharma, louder than thunder, for the third time. But roll no. 37, a proud MBBS (Member of Back Benchers Society), had something much more important on mind. Roll no. 37 was thinking how did Nupurdi manage to look so good? She was so thin, tall and fair. Everybody in the school vied for her attention.

'Can I borrow your pen?' she had asked me once. And I made sure that I gave her my favorite red pen, which she didn't return to me. I thought she loved it and proudly told all my friends that Nupurdi was using my pen. It was only later that I saw it lying near the classroom door.

She had poker straight hair and it was just the colour of ginger, whereas my hair felt like grass. Her mom let her shape her eyebrows while mine were undone. She also smelled so good always. Mom did not even let me wear perfume. I would make the wisest possible use of my only deodorant, which my aunt had got me from the US, but by the time the first class got over, I smelt like the fruit jelly or the pickle in my lunch box.

No matter how heavy the school bag, I'd try placing it on one shoulder because that's what Nupurdi did. I would pray to God for it to rain, so that I could also wear my pink sneakers with the uniform, like she did. My fringe with my tightly-oiled pony tail made me look funny and boys teased me.

Time flew and soon we both passed out of school. Nupurdi is now confined to my memories of school. The hair straightening irons, saloons, branded stores, increased pocket money, Gucci, Prada, Dolce & Gabana have changed me from roll no. 37 to 'Nupur part two'.

But the question that often haunts me: am I beautiful now or was I beautiful then?

Stutee Nag

Manisha's Gyan

It was my first day in the tenth standard and I sat in the only available place as all the other desks were occupied. The girl beside me wore thick glasses, had bushy eyebrows and plaited hair. I was happy — it meant she was not one of the Barbie types, interested only in dressing up but was focused on studies. I excitedly asked her, 'Are you good in Math?'

She smiled and said, 'Of course not. I barely manage to pass in my subjects.' My expression took a hundred-and-eighty-degree turn. I was a topper and believed that there was nothing more important in student life than to acquire knowledge and that learning could not come from anywhere else except textbooks. I muttered to myself that I would have to find a new desk partner who was bright and studious.

However as the days passed, Manisha taught me many things — like how to dribble a basketball, narrate a poem with expression, and most importantly, how to take life lightly. 'There is more to life than good marks, being a nerd and having no personality,' she commented one day.

'I have no personality?' I was shell-shocked.

'No one ever told you that before?' she burst out laughing. I could not help smiling too, though when I reached home I looked at myself for a long time in the mirror.

On my birthday she handed me a card that read, 'Want to catch all the attention ...', as I flipped to the inside written in bold letters were the words, 'then romp naked.' As I squirmed, Manisha laughed and said, 'Chill yaar, you are always so uptight. Learn to laugh at yourself.'

She also taught me not to be so self-conscious — another lesson that I now follow religiously.

Manisha was practical and would say, 'You are emotionally much stronger than you think. Give yourself credit for it and when the situation demands you will realise it for yourself.' At that time I had just shrugged it off as another one of her pearls of wisdom, or 'Manisha's gyan' as I called it.

Life has indeed tested my emotional equilibrium and each time I have emerged triumphant. I still remember Manisha, the girl whom I thought would be of no use to me but in reality, who taught me life's most important lessons.

Sanaea Patel

Phoenix

I had a diary full of letters — letters of severe criticisms and analysis of myself, my relationships, and the way I lived. This diary was my constant companion. I used to carry it everywhere and obsessively, compulsively fill it.

Once, for a group project we were at a classmate's house, who also happened to be one of the girls I disliked most in the class for being nasty to others. In midst of the work, I had switched off and found myself unscrupulously scribbling away some words of agony in my diary. After work when I reached home, I was interrupted by a phone call.

'Hey, I am sorry … but I couldn't help it, it was too tempting. I read your diary. You had left it on my bed.' As blood rushed to my face, all I could tell her was 'Okay.' A veil had been ripped apart.

The next day she returned the book with a smirk and said, 'You hate yourself, don't you?'

'Yes, I do.' The answer spread a wave of shock across her face.

The nasty girl I knew came forward to touch my hand. Perhaps to assure? Reassure? Or sympathise? I had moved back by then, refusing the gesture. I smiled at her and decided to walk away.

As I walked down the corridor, innumerable thoughts were swimming in my head about the moment that had just passed; the words I had let slip from my mouth, my words in my book, above all about myself! It was a moment of revelation. I did not love myself — my flaws, my virtues, my existence. In fact I had never considered liking myself. I was so obsessed with being cynical and pessimistic that I had never separated myself from the book. To fill the pages had become an obsession. My world was constantly being scrutinised by myself cruelly, and what was left at the end of this exercise?

How was I to live this way? How could I live my life without love? Love was important to all. But I hadn't even tried to identify it in my life. I had never looked at the beauty of my life, forget ever identifying it. I had imprisoned myself within my own cynical words.

All she did was hold a mirror before me. I smiled as I walked. Like a phoenix which burns into ashes to be reborn more colourful again, I knew my diary writing days were over. And I promised myself that I would begin with positive thoughts and a promise to love.

To begin with — loving myself….

Nisha Nair

Sin and Virtue

'Ratnadip, don't you think nowadays you are going home a little later than usual?' asked one of my colleagues who stayed with me in the same residential colony.

'I don't have a wife waiting for me at home,' I replied light-heartedly.

'But you have a little sister and a mother who might be.'

'They find me a hopelessly boring fellow,' I smiled, ignoring his nosiness.

He remained silent for some time, and then said to me, 'I am not one to interfere in other's affairs but there's a reason behind my inquisitiveness. Almost every evening when I reach home I find your sister taking walks with Mr Subramanium's father. Somehow I don't like that old man. All I can say that if I had a teenage sister, I would not let her tread his shadow. Nobody knows what suppressed desires an old man may have.'

Though I remained silent, the information hit me like a thunderbolt. I'd seen the old man a few times. He was close to seventy. I had always thought of him as a man in despair and as such harmless. I also knew Mr and Mrs Subramanium, who were respectable, religious and spiritual too.

That evening I left office at 5.20 p.m. My mind was full of thoughts about my little sister, Renu. She was tall for fourteen, with bright eyes and a broad forehead. Being more than a good twelve years older than her, I was fiercely protective of her. After my father's death last year, I had become even more so.

Every night before I went to sleep, I tiptoed to the adjacent room where Renu and my mother slept together. Seeing them sleeping comfortably gave me a strange consolation. Renu's innocent face always made me realise how vulnerable she was. This sense of responsibility was a driving force in my life.

On reaching my apartment, I saw Renu in the garden sitting cross-legged, listening to the old man sitting near her. I frowned as I saw Renu take his hand to help him stand.

They ambled from one end of the garden to the other. The old man was the speaker and Renu the listener. After a while when she came home I asked, 'Where were you?'

'Why Dada?' said my sister casually. 'I was walking with a friend.'

'This evening I reached home early and you were not there,' I said.

'So what? Now I am totally at your disposal,' said Renu, giving me a fond smile.

'Renu, you are growing up. You must always be careful in choosing your friends.' I told her. Renu remained silent, looking at me strangely as though she had read my mind.

Next evening too I reached home early. Renu was not there. Just like the previous day she came home after a while.

Every evening I decided to admonish Renu but in her presence I became tongue tied. Beneath her innocence was a strong individualism which warned me to be cautious.

One afternoon when my colleague informed me that he had seen Renu and old Subramanium having bhelpuri from a roadside stall outside our colony the previous evening, I thought it was time to talk to her.

'Renu, why do you waste your time with that old Subramanium every evening?' I asked her, almost accusingly.

She was surprised at this sudden question. 'Why Dada? What's wrong with that?' Her brows puckered slightly.

'In these formative years of your life, you should be with friends your age.' Renu did not reply immediately. She looked at me compassionately for a long moment. All of a sudden she looked much older than she was.

'First, let me correct you, Dada. Grandpa, whom you referred to as that "old Subramanium," never came to talk to me. One afternoon while I was going out I saw him sitting on a bench in front of our building. His wrinkled cheeks were wet with tears. He looked so unhappy that I went up to ask him what was wrong. At first he evaded telling me, but then he described his lonesome days here. His son and wife rarely speak to him. He is not allowed to dine with them. He has to wash his clothes by himself. Once he had soiled his trousers and since then they wouldn't let him use the washing machine. Whenever his daughter-in-law is at home, he is not supposed to come out of his room.'

Taken aback by Renu's revelation, I asked her, 'If that is so, then why doesn't he go back to his hometown?'

'He has no relatives there! I just hear him talk for he has no one else to talk to. Moreover he is a great storyteller. He has told me so many stories of Guy de Maupassant, O Henry, Tolstoy and many more,' Renu paused, and then added almost as an afterthought. 'If my own grandfather was alive, I would have wanted him to be like Subramanium grandpa.'

I remained silent, completely at a loss for words. Like most city-dwellers I too looked at everyone with suspicion, doubt and disbelief. How wrong I was to look up to Mr and Mrs Subramanium for their superficial spiritual activities and what a fool I was to think of that old man as a reprobate.

Renu might be young in years but she had much more wisdom than me and I am proud of that!

Ratnadip Acharya

The Girl in the Mirror

I look at the girl in the mirror.
Is she really me? I wonder.

Is this how I'm supposed to be?
When I'm not a polished, 'cooler' version of me?

No, I decide.
She's too weak. She probably wouldn't survive.

I need to be strong.
I need to move on.

From things that hurt,
Things that burn ...

I finally give a decisive shrug and walk off,
Pushing back the guilt inside, the conversation had brought.

A few weeks later,
Past the mirror I walk

This time, she's the one who talks.
She looks at the girl standing opposite her,
Sad, broken, crumpled and defeated in her heart …
'I thought you were strong,'
She whispered to me ....

'Yeah, maybe sometimes I'm just wrong,
And not who I'm supposed to be …'

She smiles and nods in agreement,
Her disappointment finally forgotten …

A smile appears in her cheeks round,
And she says:
'It's okay, don't let them break you down.'

I look away, in shame.
Was this the person I'd given up to get popularity and
fame?

Something gave way inside of me.
And proudly, I told her -
'Now I'm gonna be what I want to be.'

She smiles again and says:
That's what I wanted you to realise for the past few
days ....
Don't be anyone but yourself,
That's the best you can be …
And in my heart, the truth of those words I felt.

I smiled and promised her never to be fake
Never to hurt someone or be two-faced,

I'd finally accepted who I was
With all my perfections and my flaws …

Sneha Tulsian

The Runaway Student

I packed my bag like only a thirteen-year-old could.

There was no telephone, diary, water or warm clothes in the bag but I had made sure to take my sea-shell collection. It was a shoddy effort no doubt but considering it was my first experience at running away from home, I could be forgiven.

I thought about picking up the pieces of the piggy bank I had broken and then changed my mind. Why should I be nice to my parents? They had been nothing but nasty to me. Now that I had a princely sum of two hundred and fifty rupees with me, I could go anywhere I wanted and do whatever I wished.

'Nobody will scold me from now on,' I repeated to myself loudly and resolved never to come home again.

The year was 1997 and my father had just been transferred from Mumbai to a small semi-rural city in Gujarat. All of a sudden, there were too many adjustments to be made.

To make matters worse, I hated my school. Being a new student, and that too one from a big city, was enough for my classmates to bully me needlessly. The strain on me was enormous and showed in my report card.

From being a rank holder in my school in Mumbai, I had now failed miserably in three subjects in the first quarterly examinations. My parents began to get strict with me and warned me to concentrate on my studies. I felt all alone, hopeless and defeated. The only solution, as I could see it, was running away from it all.

As I slung the bag over my shoulder and tiptoed towards the door to freedom, a name came to my mind.

Susan!

My best friend in Mumbai since class one. We had grown up together and shared our dreams about the future. How could I take this step without informing her? Unfortunately the only way to contact her would be calling up my school, which also had an orphanage. Someone from there, I hoped, could give her the message.

I dialled the numbers carefully and waited for a response. After several rings, a girl picked up the phone.

'Hi, my name is Archana. I was a student there till last year. Could you please pass on a message to Susan who studies in VIII A?' I asked.

'Archana?' the voice at the other end enquired. 'Oh! It really is you! It's Jenny here.'

Jenny was a classmate of ours and a resident of the children's home. She had never been a close friend of mine but at this point I needed her to convey an important message. I said hello and got to the point.

'Jenny, I need a favour from you. Please inform Susan tomorrow, that my life is miserable here ... I ... I am completely depressed and am going to run away from home. I have money, I am going to buy a ticket to Mumbai and ....' I stopped, unsure of how to say it.

There was no response from the other end. I mustered up courage to continue.

'.... I will need to stay at her place ... till ... you know ... I just … clear things out with myself.' I whispered, afraid to hear the words I was saying. 'So will you give her the message?'

There was silence for a few seconds. 'Yes,' said Jenny finally. 'And I will also tell her what a big fool you are.'

The words hit me by surprise. Only a 'huh?' came out of my mouth.

'All my life I have waited for someone to call me and say "Jenny, your new parents are here! Someone finally wants to adopt you" but it never came. And you? You have a home, you have wonderful parents and everything one dreams of and yet you want to run away from it.'

'I don't know what problems you are going through,' she said, her voice quivering a little. 'But ... it would be difficult to be unhappy if one has a mom and a dad. I wish I had your parents and you were in my place and ... no ...I didn't mean that ... sorry ...' Jenny trailed off as some unknown emotion brought us together for the first time.

I slumped over the chair and closed my eyes as images from the past came flooding back to me. Several of my classmates were orphans and prospective adopters would often come by the school to look at them. I remembered celebrating with those who found a new home but never thought about those who were not selected. How difficult it must have been for Jenny and the others ... yet they never made a show of their hurt.

I put my hands on my head and finally allowed the tears to fall; they had been held back for too long. I wanted to apologise and thank Jenny for bringing me back to my senses but the line had already been disconnected.

Then and there, I made a decision to transform myself. After a few determined and difficult months, I soon found myself back among the rank holders in class. I actively connected with my classmates and found that they were not so bad after all. My parents were pleasantly surprised at my attitude, with my mother crediting a new 'energy drink' for the change! Little did they know the truth!

As years passed by, I never forgot Jenny or our conversation. I was not able to speak to her again as she had moved to a new city. Last heard, a nice couple from Australia had given her a home.

I keep scouring social networking sites, messaging every Jenny I see but have not found her yet. I hope she reads this someday and I get to talk to her one more time. I want to thank her from the bottom of my heart, but also to tell her that she is wrong.

She said it is difficult to be unhappy if someone has a mom and dad. I say it is impossible to be unhappy if you live with people who love you.

Archana Mohan

The Richest by Far

I think I was in the seventh grade when I met Tanya. She had come to my house with her father. They had just moved to Ahmedabad and were enquiring about school admissions. My grandfather was a trustee in the school I studied in. My father called me and introduced us; Tanya was my age and had come from Hyderabad.

Tanya started attending school after a few days, and since I was the only person she knew, we became partners and shared a common desk. I noticed that she was different from the other friends I had. There was a simplicity about her which struck me. While others cribbed about all sorts of things — from acne to homework, she seemed happy and content and never engaged in that sort of talk. But when it came to travel discussions, she joined in animatedly.

Whilst we all had traveled to exotic foreign locales, she would show us pictures of beautiful historic places like the Golconda Fort or the Hussein Sagar Lake with its towering Buddha statue and other places with the most beautiful landscapes I had ever seen. While on Mondays we boasted of the latest expensive restaurant where we had dined the previous day, her Sundays would be spent at the museum or she would have gone on a day's trek to Jambugoda or the jeep safari at Dasada.

While we had hobbies like tennis and squash, hers were gardening, sketching and reading. We would be playing with our PSP; she would be playing chess with her brother. Strangely I envied her life; it was so different from the rest of us. On my birthday whilst all my friends gave me costly gifts, she gave me the most unique handpainted card that lies pinned on my bill board even today.

One day we were assigned to do a project together. We were supposed to do it over the weekend. I insisted she come over to my house. She came after lunch and it was around five o'clock when we took a break. My cook served sandwiches and cold coffee. Then we got down to work again but couldn't complete the project as her dad came to pick her up on his way back from work.

The next day I went over to her place, little knowing that I was about to learn a lesson that no school could have taught me. I felt bewildered as I entered her house. There were no fleet of cars parked outside: only one Santro and a motor cycle. The house hardly had any furniture. The walls were white washed and there were no curtains, just brown paper stuck on the windows. Her bed had a mattress, with some cushions placed neatly on it. Her desk was a wooden bench, and stacked on it were a few books, a pencil holder with sharpened pencils and a couple of pens, which I'm sure actually worked as opposed to mine which contained numerous fancy pens, half of which were useless.

There was a mirror on one wall and on the other wall hung beautiful pictures of landscapes. Some were her sketches and some were photographs, probably from her weekend hiking trips around Hyderabad. Yet her room had such a warm and cozy feel to it!

Once we had finished our work, her mother made us the most lip-smacking onion pakodas I had ever tasted along with a cup of piping hot ginger tea.

Back home I felt ashamed of myself. In all this time I had never once realised her modest lifestyle. It's true she never once complained about anything. I marvelled at the fact that none of the things she did needed much money and yet they were all so enriching. I had so many wealthy friends but I found her to be the richest by far.

Ayushi Agarwal

Understanding My Teens

My elder daughter is watching a movie in my room. She gets so deliriously involved in it, that she seems to forget that she has had neither lunch nor breakfast, and even though her eyes are feasting, her stomach is complaining loudly. During the commercial break she reluctantly runs down, two steps at a time at full speed to grab anything edible she can lay her hands on. Imagine her fury when she sees her sister has not only taken her place but has also changed the channels. She screams at her to change the channel back but the younger one is too strong-headed to agree.

A tiff (read brawl) ensues, which my husband and I try in vain to umpire. We might as well have been invisible like Mr India. No one sees or hears us. In a flash the younger one rushes to her room, remote control in tow and locks her dresser. The older one follows close at her heels and demands the remote but she refuses to open the door. Frustrated at not getting her way, the older one slams the glass door with her fist and in seconds the entire floor is carpeted by shards of glass. So much for my cozy Sunday afternoon with family! One of them stomps out of the house angrily and the other one is sobbing, her head buried in the pillow and pieces of glass embedded in her foot. And guess what, they are both angry with me. Me? What did I do?

That night I replay the episode in my mind, and instantly I am transported to my teen days. The fights I had with my sister, no wonder I kept getting that feeling of *déjà vu* whenever my kids fight. My sister and I had cat fights. My poor mother who tried to referee our scraps got punched by mistake on more than a couple of occasions. Back then our fights entailed hitting and scratching, clawing and biting compared to modern day teenage fights which involve hiding valuable assignments, formatting the rival computer, spying and smashing glasses to smithereens …. Suddenly I burst out laughing recalling the dazed look on my mother's face when a day after the 'big war' my sister and me would be sharing a joke and laughing, much to her chagrin.

I remember always being on edge as a teen, life was a rollercoaster ride and there were countless growing pains. The boy I was eyeing didn't know I existed and the nerdy guy gave more attention than I could handle. Then there was always the shortage of funds; pocket money was never enough and we had to think of innovative ways to save money, having chai at the canteen as opposed to coffee at the Taj. Clothes, oh my god! There never seemed enough of those. The cupboard would be me overflowing but getting up every morning and thinking of what to wear gave enough blood pressure akin to what an adult has before a board meeting.

Once when my mom forced me to organise my cupboard, I found clothes which I wore when I was ten, not to forget the half eaten burger that fell out too! Imagine after how many years I must have cleaned it. If my memory serves me right I had enough clothes to become the biggest donor during the floods in Andhra.

Friends were another reason for stress. There were too many cliques with too many conditions to comply with before joining any of them. Similar to taking up a job if you ask me — the wrong choice and you are done for!

The fact that as a teen I hated the food my mom cooked cannot be eschewed either. She took extra efforts to cook what would please me, but I would knock it without giving a second thought and order a dosa from Santosh Sagar. After a grilling day at college I could definitely do without the unforgiving glare my dad gave me.

Oh, and the academic system, they were designed solely for our torture. Every few months there was a board exam or preliminary or term paper. What the heck! As if life isn't hard without them. Our report presentation in the AGM is a piece of cake compared to those.

Suddenly I feel sympathetic toward my kids. Looking back at my own teen days I realise they were tough, they prepared you for adulthood, and they were trying and testing times. Any relationship that outlasts our teen age has passed all test of time and will be with us till our last moment. There was too much to deal with. A smile crosses my face; one thing about that age is that we always live in the present. We never have time to dwell on the past or worry about what problems tomorrow can bring. We just know that the only happy moment in the present. We all forget this important lesson in our journey to adulthood. All said and done, my most cherished memories are of those days filled with heartaches, headaches, and the works. Nothing can replace them. No amount of books on pop psychology or philosophy can teach you what you learnt in your adolescence.

As sure as sunrise, my kids are on back-slapping terms again and yesterday's fracas will remain in memory only till the broken glass is replaced.

This is the power of now!

Shashi Agarwal

Vijay Sir

Awaiting the results of my twelvth boards had not been as stressful. I stared at the computer screen to see if I had been selected for the best design institute in the city. Yes! I had made it! I was on cloud nine, all my hard work had paid off.

Finally, the big day dawned. The orientation was promising and the teachers seemed amiable. Only Vijay Sir seemed less than friendly.

In the first week itself, we were overloaded with assignments. On the third day of college I attended Vijay Sir's lecture and I was right, he was rather strict and it was apparent that he liked taking us to task with a vengeance. He would commission the most arduous tasks.

One Friday I spent the entire night making models for our assignment. I barely managed to complete them by Saturday afternoon. I submitted my project and went home tired, and immediately crashed into bed. Instead of going out in the weekend, I slept through most of it.

Come Monday morning, I went to college. The first lecture was Vijay Sir's, and I was less than five seconds late, but he still threw me out of the class. I was almost in tears. In the recess he called me to his office and rubbished my entire assignment. I had to redo it by Friday, which meant more sleepless nights. I was ready to break down. Shaken, I retreated to my class, lest I be embarrassed further by crying in front of my batchmates.

In every class, he would find fault with whatever I had done. Either the measurement was wrong or the layout or the elevation, I just could not seem to get it right. Every night I would cry myself to sleep wondering what misconceptions had made me even apply for this stream. I started loathing Vijay Sir for his hostility and the torture he inflicted on me. What really upset me was that I had spent hours preparing the project but he had slammed it in seconds. Wasn't it worth a second look? Could he not give us even a little room to grow?

The coming weeks went by in a haze of gruelling hard work and nights spent on the drafting tables in college. The other teachers were pretty laidback and would allow us latitude, except for this one teacher who was so hard to please.

It was another manic Monday and as usual I was four seconds late and it was Vijay Sir's class. I knew I would not be allowed in and I silently berated myself for being late again. When I entered the class, I was not stopped. Surprised and happy, I quickly went to my bench. We had faculty visiting from Germany that day. Sir was showing them around and suddenly he came and stood before my desk. He asked me to fetch my draft sheets. My heart racing, I went to my locker and got them. He showed them to the professors and pointed out how precise my work was. The lines were clear and definable, he said. I almost fainted; nothing would have prepared me for his praise. My day was made; I walked ten feet tall that entire day.

In the next class however, my submission was again rejected. Back to hating Vijay Sir and his dictatorship, I braced myself for the drill. Apart from the sporadic commendation I got, time crept along. I felt worn out and encumbered with work.

One night, I was working at the drafting table with a couple of friends. After some time we decided to go to the chaiwalla on the street outside. The light was on in Vijay Sir's office, and I peeked in. I am so thankful I did, because it changed my life forever. Vijay Sir was sitting behind his desk with a pile of submissions in front of him. He was measuring each one of them meticulously for precision. He looked tired and weary and I went inside and offered him a cup of tea. He smiled and I felt an indescribable flutter of jubilation. Sir joined us for tea.

Somehow, just the realisation that he worked so hard to correct our work made it worth the effort. He explained that technical drawing allowed no margin for inaccuracy, which understandably made him the enemy. He was aware of that, but he wanted to hone designers, not start a fan club.

In that moment of awe, I understood it was time to grow up and take our work seriously. I threw out any fancy notions I had of easy college life and along with it banished my intention to drop out the coming year.

Anushka Agarwal

8

PAINFUL PARTINGS

The world is round and the place which may seem like the end may also be the beginning.

—Ivy Baker Priest

Adieu

In my teen years, I was always in awe of people who I used to adore from afar and could think of nothing better than being friends with them. So for me it was with Suchitra, a girl in my colony. She was pretty and there seemed to radiate from her a very pleasant aura. Whenever I saw her, I would want to befriend her but my feelings of inferiority held me back.

Suchitra seemed unaware of her own beauty; I had heard nice things about her from the girls who lived nearby. When I told one of them that I would like to meet her, she said, 'Just smile at her, she will smile back and you will be friends.' That simple!

I was just hanging out in the park one day, when I saw Suchitra walking in my direction … I decided to follow my friend's advice and smiled hesitantly at her. Suchitra smiled back warmly and from that day on we started talking to each other. After a few days, she asked me to teach her how to play badminton and I readily agreed. I was keen to have her as a friend and what better opportunity could I have asked for? We started playing every evening. This brought us really close, and very soon we started sharing our secrets, problems and even started studying together. In our free time we would go window shopping or to the movies or simply listen to music. We practically spent the whole day together.

After a few months I started getting bored of her. The newness of the friendship wore off and the things I had liked about her started irritating me. I started feeling claustrophobic because she would show up constantly at my place. Her relaxed sense of familiarity annoyed me further and I would try to avoid her. But she remained unperturbed even when I was angry with her.

One Thursday afternoon, she told me she was going away for the weekend to meet her grandparents and would be back the next Monday. Hearing this strangely gave me immense relief. Come Monday she didn't turn up but I didn't think much of it but by Tuesday I missed her company and I grudgingly admitted to myself that she meant more to me than I gave her credit for. Maybe she was avoiding me because I had been rude to her on more than one occasion.

The next day morning, however, when there was no news of her, I started to worry and decided to go over to her place and apologise for my conduct. Outside her house were a group of people talking in hushed whispers and even before anyone could tell me what had happened, I knew something was terribly wrong. I ran into the house and stopped abrubptly when I saw Suchitra and her mother lying on the floor, motionless, covered in white sheets. I was too shocked to react or cry. I remembered vaguely reading in the paper about a train accident the previous day. My head started spinning and I felt faint.

Days went by and I yearned for her company; nothing anyone said would console me. She had been my best friend and I could not comprehend my appalling behaviour towards her. How rightly the Bard has said, *'We look before and after, and pine for what is not.'*

After that, I was scared of making friends, my studies deteriorated and I lost interest in all my hobbies. I just could not come to terms with the fact that she was no more.

After a few months her father sold their house and moved away. The lock on the door was like a sign indicating the end of a chapter. This had a cathartic effect on me; It signified that I too should lock my memories of her and move ahead. That same night I saw Suchitra in my dreams, waving me goodbye. I woke up the next morning feeling invigorated. I was ready to face the world again, this time armed with the knowledge of a well-lerned lesson — good friends may sometimes be annoying when they are around but the vacuum they leave when they go away is too overwhelming to endure.

Tammana Pant

He Was My Happiest Hello and Hardest Goodbye

There are some people whom you always want to have in your life … forever. Yes, these special people are our very dear friends and we really never want to lose them. They are like kites flying in the sky, each attached to us by a string. They soar high in the sky and make it as colourful as ever. They are always there for us and make our lives happy and worth living. But even kites don't stay attached to us for long. Sometimes they get lost and can never be found again!

Aditya and I had been friends from class eight. He was the first friend I made after my family shifted to Kolkata. I still remember the day I met him. It was my first day in The Heritage School, I was kind of nervous when I came to the bus stand with my dad. Under a huge tree was my bus stand, where a boy stood, wearing the same uniform as mine. His sparkling eyes and smile showed only one thing — mischief.

'Hey, are you new? he asked me with a shy grin.

'Yeah. It's my first day. I'm Agniv,' I introduced myself.

'Aditya,' the boy replied.

We both looked at each other and smiled. He told me that he too was in class eight. At that time, I did not know that this stranger would become one of the most important person in my life.

Aditya was quite an ordinary boy in school, but cracked the best jokes. His peculiar way of laughing made them even funnier. He took life very casually and hardly cared for anything. I barely had anything in common with him. But we bonded through laughter and our love for football. Even though he wasn't really outstanding in studies, Aditya had a remarkable talent for football. At an early age, he had proved that he could be 'someone' with his skill.

We both were always there for each other. We laughed and celebrated our happiness and also shared each other's sadness. He was like the sibling I never had.

Every day at school we used to sit, chat and crack jokes, irrespective of what the teachers had to say to us. The lunch break was a very important time in our daily schedule. We would usually be in the same team despite protests from others. Everyone knew that the Aditya-Agniv duo was the deadliest. We were therefore considered the 'Double Charge' — the duo who could never let a team lose. The periods after lunch usually left me with the great responsibility of waking him up each time he got caught by a teacher for dozing off.

After school dispersed, we usually talked about cars, footballers and their clubs during our bus ride home. If there was one thing that Aditya would readily study, it was about football and cars. He knew almost every car in the world, their manufacturer, engine and all those complicated stuff you usually study in engineering. And in football, ranging from the weight of a standard football to the height of Cristiano Ronaldo — he knew it all. Every alternate Friday, we treated each other with a choco bar from the nearby ice cream parlour. Even on weekends, we used to go to each other's house to hang out. As exams approached, we both became equally tense since we had hardly opened our textbooks during the year to study.

Yes, like this Aditya filled my life with many memories worth remembering. The most memorable of them, came in the last day of Class Eight....

That day was a Friday and Aditya was not his usual self; his smile was missing when I met him at the bus stop. His eyes lacked that spark of excitement.

'Is anything wrong?' I asked him in the bus.

'No, I'm fine,' he said.

I didn't believe him and retorted, 'Tell me, man! Maybe I can help you.' But Aditya sat quietly without a saying a word.

In class he sat lifelessly, lost in some other world. He seemed deeply troubled about something, which he would not tell anyone. Even at break, he sat in one corner of the field with that sad face of his. It didn't suit him at all. My friends and I couldn't take it anymore.

'What do you think of us? Do we mean nothing to you?' we said angrily after break. 'If you don't tell us what's wrong, you can jolly well get out of our group!'

Aditya looked at us and we were shocked to see that his eyes were red and tears rolled down his round cheeks. Immediately, I sat beside him and asked gently, 'Tell us, Aditya, we know something is seriously wrong.'

'I'm leaving school!' he blurted out. 'I pleaded with my parents, but they wouldn't listen! I'm moving to the US!' He was sobbing harder now.

The whole world suddenly started to spin for me. The bell rang and slowly my friends bid him farewell and wished him a good life ahead. Aditya too smiled for the first time. In the bus, he seemed quite normal. I was the one who was quiet now. I thought about all the fun I'd had with him and how it was going to end now.

As we got down from the bus, I looked at Aditya.

'So this is it, brother? We walk on two different roads now. I am really going to miss you.'

'Me too! I will never forget you. Ever,' he said smiling while tears rolled down his eyes.

We hugged each other and said bye for one final time. But Aditya turned around, and said bye again, and then again and again … as if he knew he would never say it to me again.

As he crossed the road and went into his complex, I realised that it was a Friday and I had forgotten to treat him to a choco bar. Well, now it didn't matter anymore.

I still wonder how someone, who was once a stranger, made me cry so much. Well, even though now we are on two different sides of the globe, Aditya is still very close to me. Though there is Facebook and the telephone, his string is not attached to me anymore. My brother is now far away from me. He was really my happiest hello and hardest goodbye.

Agniv Basu

Irrevocable

'Dream as if you'll live forever, live as if you'll die today.'
This is how I have chosen to live my life.

I had a friend Mehrunissa, who studied with me in school.
She would get chocolates for me every day and always tried
to help me out in whatever ways she could. Even though
I considered her one of my good friends, I never gave her
much importance or time.

On the last day of school, she invited me for lunch to her
house, which was a long drive from the city. I wasn't very
keen to go but I obliged, as I did not want to disappoint
her. Her parents, brother and sisters made me feel very
important, not that I deserved it.

After passing out from school, we went to different
colleges. It became almost impossible to meet, but she
would write to me regularly despite my erratic replies to
her letters.

Six months later, one day just when I was about to board
a bus, I saw Mehrunissa. She was walking towards the bus
stop and had not seen me. The bus was about to leave and I
had to decide between leaving, or missing my bus to talk to
her and then take the next bus. I chose to leave though I felt

a little bad doing it, but I told myself that there was always a next time.

After ten days I got a letter from her saying that it had been a long time and we should get together. However, the postscript at the end of her letter read disaster. It was in a different handwriting. It said that Mehrunissa had written this letter to be posted to me but she was now battling for her life in the neighbourhood hospital. The electricity pole in front of her house had fallen on her, during the heavy rains, and she had to be admitted into hospital and was in the ICU.

I was shocked. Along with my parents, I rushed to the hospital. Mehrunissa was in a critical state and no visitors were allowed to meet her. Her chances of survival were very bleak. After two days, she passed away.

I was shattered and overcome with deep regret.

Ever since, I have not been able to forgive myself for putting off meeting her. If only I could get another chance, I would make up for all the time I had avoided spending with her. But alas! I realised the value of her friendship only after she was gone!

That was a turning point for me when I learnt that life rarely gives a second chance, so when we have one, we should make the most of it. I have learnt to appreciate friendship and cherish the times spent with my friends.

Reshmi A.R.

Light and Shadow

Light and shadow playing hide and seek
Among rippling waters and grassy banks
Bring to mind those bygone memories
Of the tugging of pigtails
And billowing skirts
Crinkling of eyes against the sun
Leaning against an ancient tree
Snatching of chocolates
Sharing of a single orange bar
Amongst three friends.

Light and shadow playing hide and seek
Bring to mind those lazy afternoons
Of graduating from Enid Blytons
Into the world of Mills & Boons.
Of waking at mornings with a longing heart
Of spending nights in pillowed tears
Of settling dupattas against the naughty wind
Of eyes averted while passing boys at the kerb
Of whispers and giggles
Amongst three friends.

Light and shadow playing hide and seek
With every turn of life I took
Headstrong decisions and regret pangs
Those flights of fancy, impossible to fathom now
Teenage dreams and desperations
Inevitable then, bring a wistful smile
As each step strengthened on rugged paths
And each time the world was a little more
Mine and only mine
In the parting of three friends.

Monika Pant

My First Love

I woke up to the alert tone of a message on my mobile phone. It was a bright Saturday morning and I had just woken up. I ignored the message and walked to the bathroom to wash my face. After drinking a glass of water, I then casually checked my mobile. My sleepy face suddenly brightened and I jumped with joy. It was Mark, one of my best friends, who had messaged me. He was back from the United States of America!

Mark had left a year ago, to study abroad after completing high school. I had missed him so much and was very glad that he was back. He had already made plans to meet up that afternoon at Ben's house, my other best friend and a good friend of Mark's too. I couldn't wait!

The afternoon finally arrived and I ran to Ben's house, as we lived close by. I walked into Ben's room and there was Mark. He rushed to greet me and gave me the tightest hug ever! We hugged for almost five minutes and Ben had to separate us. We looked like clowns as our smiles would just not be wiped off from our faces! Indeed it was a memorable afternoon.

A week later was my high school prom and I was taking Mark as my date, since Ben was graduating with me. We didn't know whether to be happy or sad, because I was to leave for India the day after the prom, though I was coming back two weeks later. Even though it was just for a week, I felt sad.

Prom night finally arrived and we all had a great time. But there were two people who had the best time of their lives, and that was Mark and me. We took pictures, and he got along well with my friends and we sat and just chatted. He was the perfect gentleman. As we left the ballroom, Mark held my hand and then I knew that everything felt right. It just hit me then that the small moments Mark and I had shared throughout our lives, such as fighting over chocolates, eating out of each other plates, watching movies on the couch, calling each other up at 2 a.m. just because we wanted to talk, teasing each other and many more, was what people call 'love'. I was too scared to express these feelings for him.

When I left for India the next day, I wanted Mark to know how I felt, but couldn't tell him. I didn't know what to do.

But when I reached India, I checked my mail, and to my shock and surprise, Mark had written a long mail, telling me that he had similar feelings for me. I regretted coming to India without telling him how I felt about him. I was happy, yet sad that he was in Zambia and I was in India, and we had expressed our feelings without seeing each other.

The week I was in Zambia, after I returned, was one I would never forget. It went by so fast that I did not even realise it. My heart tore apart when I saw Mark for the last time. He came home that night. The house was bare, empty and quiet. His head was on my lap and we looked into each other's eyes. I held back my tears. We talked for hours. We really wanted this relationship to work, but we both knew it wouldn't. It would be hard as he would be in America and I would be in India. Our final decision was to break up.

He walked to his car and I stood at the entrance of our house, holding on to the door knob. He gestured with his hand, beckoning me to walk to him. I stared at him, heartbroken. He walked to me, put his arm around my waist and led me to his car. He looked into my eyes and said, 'I love you. This is going to be the hardest thing ever!' He gave me a long, tight hug and stepped into his car. He drove off, leaving me alone on the cold and empty driveway. I felt tears in my eyes. I did not sleep that night.

I knew it would never work out. Long distant relationships are those that work only if the couple are truly, madly and deeply in love with each other. I was madly in love with him, but I wasn't sure if he felt the same way. But what warmed my heart was that he had once thought of me as the 'special one' in his life, and for now, that's all that mattered. Mark was, is, and will always be the first and only love of my life.

Anupama Subramaniyam

Tomorrow

'You never have time for me and I don't think I am ever going to talk to you again!' Disha yelled at me and banged down the phone. I smiled. 'I'll call her tomorrow and sort it out. She'll come around ... she always does,' I thought to myself. But little did I know that Disha's words were uncannily true.

Disha was my best friend. We attended different colleges, had different goals in life, and were far removed from each other but got along like a house on fire. Disha believed in living life to the fullest and despite studying only when examinations loomed over her head, was a good student. I, on the contrary, would go into a self-imposed exile a month before my examinations. There would be no outings and no phone calls for me, which is why Disha dreaded my exams more than I did.

I was studying for my last English paper when Disha called. We hadn't met and had hardly spoken in the last one month and she wanted me to go over to her house. It was a language paper and there wasn't much to study, but I refused. What was her urgency anyway? We could meet the next day or any day afterwards. I shudder every time I recall the desperation in her voice when she said 'When will you understand that life is short? By the time you learn to live, it will be too late!' Disha would use this line very frequently with me and I would always brush her aside.

The next morning I was up early to revise my syllabus. It was 5 a.m. when the doorbell rang. Who could it be at this hour? I stepped out of my room only to see my mother running to open the door. It was Dad. Where was he coming back from? I didn't even know that he had gone out. I felt a chill go down my spine and my hands and feet turned numb.

'Mom, Dad …what happened? Dad …where were you?' I asked feebly, almost not wanting to hear the answer. Mom looked pale and disconcerted as she walked up to me and held me tightly in her arms. I'm so sorry, darling …' she murmured.

'What are you sorry about, Mom … please tell me … tell me now!' I was almost screaming. Mom took me into my room and asked me to sit down. She stroked my head with trembling hands and said, 'Sweetheart, there are some people who are so special that even God does not want to share them with us. He sends them to earth to spread joy and after a while, calls them back….'

'Mom, who are you talking about?' I interrupted nervously.

'Disha …she is no more …' her words trailed off as I felt my head reeling before I fainted. When I regained consciousness, I was lying on my bed and my parents were sitting beside me. I was in shock and kept staring at the walls. My mother kept telling me to cry and vent out all my emotions, but I was in a state of disbelief and shock.

Close to midnight, my father had received a call. There had been an accident and the victims required blood transfusion immediately. My father was the head of an NGO that organised regular blood donation camps. He made several phone calls to arrange for the blood required and rushed to the hospital. But it was too late. There were five girls in the car that had crashed and only two of them survived. It was then that Dad got to know that one of the deceased was my friend, Disha. She had gone out for a drive with four of her friends. While the other two had died on the spot, Disha battled for her life for a couple of hours before she succumbed.

As Dad narrated the occurrences of the fateful night to me, I broke down and wept uncontrollably.

At her funeral, I stood quietly in a corner. Disha's parents, sisters and other family members were wailing, but I could not hear anything. Disha's words resounded constantly in my ears. Suddenly, the urgency in her voice when we had our last conversation began to make sense. It was almost like she had a premonition.

Disha was like a shining star and brought a lot of lustre in the lives of people who knew her. I have changed since she passed away; I know I can never be like her but I have learnt to be more cheerful and live for today — after all who knows about tomorrow?

Swati Rajgharia

We Were Just Kids

I still remember the first time I met them. We were just moving into our flat. The apartment door was open and packed boxes were scattered all around. Mum was busy with the house-warming ritual of boiling milk on the stove. I didn't understand much of what was going on — I must have been in the Fifth Standard. There were no guests, just our family and a few cousins. There was a box of sweets though and I remember walking out of the kitchen, munching a piece. There they were — peering in cautiously at the front door, with all the curiosity of a bunch of primary school boys. I suppose I was told to offer then sweets and I remember holding out the box to them. The boy from F2 below broke off a small piece politely and ate it. The one from next door, F5, took a whole sweet with an impish grin lighting up his face.

Of course, we soon became a gang. The boy from F5 had a younger sister too, whom he took care of and tormented with equal enthusiasm. They would call out to me from their verandah and I'd go to ours to chat to them. We made our plans that way, talking through the metal grill that kept us from tumbling out. We all went to different schools, but on evenings and weekends, we'd gather the rest of the kids in the apartment complex and go to the terrace to play. Bugging the watchman was a favourite game. We also made up a lot of conspiracies and had fun pretending we knew a lot more than we did.

Our games were odd — it mostly involved running around like crazy. Occasionally, we played sane games like running and catching or hide and seek. We climbed up the water tank and tried to pluck tiny mangoes. We went to the most unreachable places for an adult (like the narrow spot between the motor shed and the house) and carried on with our make-believe world. Sometimes,we had picnics on the terrace. Most of all, we were united in hating the kids in the apartment opposite ours. There was no reason. We hated them because they were there, I think. They also did tend to put up silly plays and stage fashion shows with dupattas draped around themselves. We stood at our terrace and jeered at them. Unkind, but we were kids.

Apartments are a rich source of politics. They have association meetings where they argue over whose kid broke what and who should pay for what repair and complain about the watchman's negligence and hold lengthy conversations about the upcoming water scarcity. Then there were tussles amongst people staying on rent and those who owned their apartments. We kids knew somehow if any of our parents didn't get along with each other. Those kids would stay away from each other too or probably they were made to. We had a tough time when our friend's relatives came visiting with their kids. Suddenly they would want to hang out with their cousins

and forgot us. It was hard — but we were kids with short
memory spans. That helped. Our little gang went through
all of that as well.

A few years later, both families moved away. It was weird
— not having any more playmates. But, after a while others
moved in — kids who went to the same school as I did. We
became the new terrace gang. There were more girls now
and we were older and conscious of being teenagers. We
mostly sat around the terrace, idly chatting. The boys were
younger who devised their own games now. We still made
fun of the kids in the opposite apartment, though.

There was a weekend when we were on the terrace as
usual — wandering around, looking at the world, from
our perch three floors above the road. A new boy walked
in and like kids all over the world, we stared at him
unabashed. Was he moving in? We hadn't seen any trucks
laden with furniture all day. But we made no move to talk
to him or even smile at him. We just stared and continued
wandering around. To our surprise, he followed us to the
other side as well and stood there, leaning against the
water tank, watching us. There was something intense
about the way he looked at us — not the trying-to-be
casual look of a new kid who wants to join the gang. For
about half an hour, he hung around — a little distance
away from us and we ignored him. He met my glance a few
times and held his gaze steadily. I looked away, puzzled.
When I looked back up, I heard a voice calling out from
below — I couldn't hear what was said, but someone was
calling him. He left the terrace and I heard him run down
the flights of stairs. Something clicked — maybe it was the
voice, or his gait or that familiar rhythmic rush down the

stairs. And I was running too, leaving four very puzzled people behind.

'Hari!' I called out as I ran down the stairs. I could never match his pace even two years back. I kept calling out his name till I reached the ground floor and realised he had already left. It wasn't my fault. He looked different. He could have spoken to me. It had been so long. But even back then I knew, it was cruel of me to forget.

Malavika Thiagaraja

9

SPREADING YOUR WINGS

Until you spread your wings, you'll have no idea how far you can fly.

—Unknown

Impossible is Nothing

The 21st of June, 2010. A day I can never forget. It was the day of our school's Inter House Football competition. Our house had qualified the previous day and was in the finals. I, being the captain of the team, could not miss this match. Unfortunately, that very day, I was down with 103-degree fever.

That morning at home, there was a huge argument about my going to school. Much to my dismay, my grandfather and parents won, forcing me to stay at home. I had to stay in bed all day covered with a blanket, allowed only to sit up for my meals.

Throughout the day I kept on thinking about my team and the match. Our House had some of the best players, but one of them was injured; if I too did not show up, we would surely lose the finals. The fact that we could have won would make me regret it a lot. But what finally got me into action was a phone call from school — the call came from my classmate, a good friend, pleading to be taken on the team though he couldn't play very well. I remember the words that struck fear in my heart.

'Why haven't you come today? The entire opposition

team is present here. As it is Raghvendra is injured. Now you, Ishan and Rishabh are absent too!'

On hearing these words, all my hopes of winning the match faded away. Ishan, Raghvendra and Rishabh were good players. It was as though half our team was absent! I explained to him about my health, and after putting down the phone, made a dozen calls trying to convince Mom and Dad who were away at work.

But it seemed useless. No matter how hard I tried, they just wouldn't listen. I just felt like getting up and walking out, but the fever had me bound. Finally, right before my lunch I made one last desperate attempt to convince my parents to allow me to play for the sake of my team.

To my surprise and delight, Dad allowed me to go, perhaps understanding how important it was for me. The world suddenly felt warmer (no pun intended) and I began saying a hundred thank you's to my parents. The plan was to leave at 2 o' clock and reach school just before the match started. My mother asked me to take a strong medicine that would keep the fever at bay. So, at the sound of the clock striking two, I set off for school. The medicine seemed to do the trick. I started sweating in the car, and I felt the energy rush through my veins. I took off my jacket ready to play, just as the car screeched to a halt in front of the gate.

The five-minute walk to the field wasn't eventful but as I entered the field I saw the two teams lined up on the sides with the referee. I kept walking, waiting to see what would happen, careful not to run, in case the fever took hold again.

I felt all eyes on me; some had angry eyes, some held a look of disbelief. My friends came up and asked how I was. But the real welcome was yet to come. As I walked towards the team, I raised my hand and the whole team screamed their lungs out! It felt like I was Lionel Messi, being welcomed on the field by fans! I quickened my pace and pulled on my boots, while the rest of the team patted my back and smiled at me.

Then the toss was taken and the whistle blew, signalling the start of the match. The first few minutes were like any other match, but then suddenly I noticed something was wrong. My stamina was weakening and my knees began to ache. The sun was beating down with full force; and, as my whole body screamed for rest, my mind willed me to play.

The other team seemed to have the upper hand. I couldn't run fast enough. Thankfully Ishan had been able to make it after all, and I got some support in the attack. We avoided some goals due to our strong defence. The other team's passing was better than ours and they got more possession of the ball. Thankfully the half-time whistle blew just as I was about to collapse.

Drinking a glass of water mixed with Glucon D, a senior student and I cheered up the team saying that only one half was over. But inside, I sighed. I was the captain and if we lost this time, I would never be able to forgive myself. Surprisingly that's exactly when my knees stopped aching.

It was our centre this time and when the whistle blew, I passed the ball to Ishan who gave me a through pass past an opponent. On receiving, I moved past another defender, only to see the goal blocked by two more players. I didn't want to let go of this one chance by using my usual dribble to goal strategy; and so I closed my eyes and shot.

I wasn't really one for taking shots because they weren't always accurate. But this time I don't know what happened, for when I opened my eyes, the team was screaming and jumping on me. I had scored a goal! Reinforced with new-found hope, we played on. Goal after goal was scored with accurate passing and great teamwork. A few collisions occurred including one where I crashed into an opponent but without any serious consequences.

And then it was all over ... the whistle blew with the final score 3-2 in our favour. Everyone went crazy. A few people came and congratulated me, but otherwise nobody saw me walk out of the field, across the school and into my car. With the day coming to an end, I suddenly began to shiver. The fever was coming back but I had learnt a valuable lesson that day — nothing is impossible!

Advay Pal

Speaking Out

I was meeting my kid sister after six months; actually my cousin, the pert and pretty 'Pinky', with the prettiest rosy, pink cheeks which came from living in the hills. The brat who had howled in the middle of Mall road in Shimla so loudly that her parents had no option but to buy her all the toys she wanted. The little girl who refused to eat till her daddy told her a new story, even when she was ten-years-old.

Of course I knew things would be different now since she had recently lost her dad, and a month ago, her mother had moved abroad for better job prospects. Her brother had gone with their mother, but Pinky, being the older sibling, was not taken along to prevent her from missing a year in school. My aunt wanted to be sure she had made the right move before she uprooted her fourteen-year-old daughter. So it was decided that Pinky was going to be living with her grandparents and spend all her vacations with us.

Before we went to pick her up, my mother called my brother and me to explain how we needed to be patient with Pinky, and handle her with kid gloves. We were not to get upset if they paid her more attention. I was sixteen and felt like I knew it all. Why was Mom stating the obvious? Of course we would be sensitive, and honestly how much could Pinky have changed in a few months, I thought.

I was in for a shock. Pinky was a totally changed person; the spark was gone from her eyes, she looked lost and sad. Her gait was much slower, her voice, smile everything seemed different. It was frightening. She hadn't just changed; she seemed like an older person who had given up hope. Mom held her close, Dad and my brother cracked silly jokes while I was silent on the drive back home.

Pinky and I were sharing a room and when we were alone, we started talking. I asked her what was wrong but she retorted saying, 'What is right?' There was so much bitterness in her that it was scary. She was hurt and blocking in all the pain.

The next couple of days, it was like we were all walking on egg shells, not knowing what would bring about a fresh bout of sobs. Pinky was hesitant and only spoke when spoken to. This was so disconcerting, because I could remember Mom yelling at both of us to stop giggling and talking. Now every conversation was measured. Often I saw Mom abruptly leave the table and knew she was going to the bathroom to cry. Dad was a lot more silent and I hated it.

On the way to school, my brother commented that the atmosphere at home was getting to him — it was almost like Pinky was making us feel guilty for having our parents with us ...

Pinky started becoming defiant and really began pushing her luck with me. She knew I hated anyone touching my things without my permission. Yet everyday when I got back from school, either my clothes were messed up or my books. She looked at me as if daring me to accuse her. And if I did, she would pull out the sympathy card and start crying. She was trying my patience and I spoke to my mother about it. At night she would want the lights off just as I prepared to read. Although I also felt awful about her situation, I knew that someone had to do some straight talking with her. Dad agreed with me, yet no one had the heart to say anything to the poor girl.

One morning over breakfast she commented about a newspaper report on suicide saying that the person was lucky to be away from all the pain. Everyone became sentimental and started fawning over her. I wasn't amused and walked away. My brother followed me; he understood what I was feeling. It was ridiculous and we analysed the situation threadbare. He felt that perhaps I was a little jealous since we were both girls and almost the same age. I thought about it and realised that helping Pinky was far more important than jealousy, and honestly I did not for a moment want to be where she was. She was getting into a negative spiral and we had to help her. So, we agreed on something for once and marched right back into the house.

Pinky got defensive as soon as I started talking. Tears welled-up in her eyes. Dad put a protective arm around her. I tried to be as calm as possible and started by telling everyone that I loved Pinky and wanted her to be the old fun-loving, lovely sister I had. I did not know or like this manipulative, confused Pinky that she had became. Pinky started screaming and said the most awful things, like wishing my father dead and my mother abandoning us to know what it felt like! My brother put a warning hand on my shoulder and I refused to react. I could see my parents squirming and knew that Dad was getting angry. I begged them to stay out of this and trust the fact that I had Pinky's best interests at heart.

So we let her vent. She was angry with God, with her father for dying, with her mother for going away, with her brother for accompanying her mother, with my father for not stopping her mom, and with me for not insisting that she move Mumbai. All of us were shocked; we realised that she had never told anyone all this! She said she hated the pity she got from people. She wanted to grow up right now and get a job or just marry some rich man! She wanted to run away and join some religious group or kill herself. I asked my parents to leave the room and thankfully they trusted me, and left.

I told her she was being silly and couldn't expect to live on sympathy all her life. People would start avoiding her. I remember her dad, my favourite uncle, would always say: 'Nobody owes you anything in this world. You are responsible for your happiness or unhappiness.' She was stumped to hear that. She cried and this time we could see the change.

Both of us hugged each other and cried for the longest time. My brother tried to lighten the situation and promised to be there for us. When she felt better she apologised and said she hated behaving the way she had been of late.

Later on the family bonded over a huge tub of Bavarian chocolate ice-cream, and it was decided that Pinky would move to Mumbai in two months after that term. She would study in my school and live with us, and my aunt was informed about the arrangement. For the first time in a week, Pinky smiled and began making demands. For starters, she wanted a family holiday before school began!

Shifa Maitra

The Winning Shot

Breaking up wasn't easy. It hurt too much, sending me into bouts of depression and failed attempts at trying to kill myself (failed because they were insincere attempts, thankfully!). I had given up cricket, which was my passion, and was not talking to anyone. My teen years were about to end, with my twentieth birthday around the corner, I wanted to reform myself ... I wanted myself back ... but how?

After we broke up, I got rid of my entire collection of photographs with her, deleted the ones on the computer and did away with a few accounts on social networking sites. It was a numbing process and I was filled with vengeance. After eleven months of separation, I introspected about the reasons why I could not sustain the relationship. It could have been possessiveness or even jealousy about her 'superior' performance. I kept getting 'D' grades while she managed to notch up a series of 'A's, though studying almost the same time as I did.

Indeed, I had failed. One fine day, just a week before my twentieth birthday, I was suddenly curious to find out what she was up to. The only way to know was to visit her online profile and updates.

I clicked on her profile icon, and was overcome by a strange feeling of anger. Her update read: 'Yippee! I got selected to study at my dream university in the UK!' Needless to say, fifty odd people had 'liked' that! I did not. I saw her picture ... she looked ecstatic. Soon, she would be flying away, far away from me. What was I to do? Feel enraged and shout at her with jealousy? Do a 'cry baby' act by downing some vodka? Call her and wish her an insincere 'good luck'? No ... none of those.

On my birthday I logged into my account on the site and was greeted by hundreds of birthday wishes. It was wonderful going through each one of them, but the biggest surprise was the message from her: 'Happy Birthday! Wish you all the success and hope that we meet again one day!' The message was as sincere as it could be. I felt a tug in my heart and was compelled to think beyond hate, anger and jealousy. For the first time in life, I began to understand how one could be happy about others' achievements. It was difficult, but not impossible. I remembered the lovely times I had spent with her.

I smiled slowly and felt my anger leaving me My iron grip on the computer mouse relaxed. I opened the curtains and the windows to let in fresh air and sunshine. I saw her smiling profile once again and smiled back at her. Turning off the computer, I took my cricket bat and went for the scheduled match.

There I was, hitting the best shots I could, and as the ball soared up, I saw a British Airways plane in the sky. Instead of resentment, I felt happiness. I had grown up. My life was now in my hands. I was finally going to throw away my grudges and concentrate on the path ahead. I looked around — my friends were cheering too, it was a straight six ... in fact, it was the winning shot!

Ram Kumar Swamy

To Fly

One of the most difficult things to do while growing up is making your own decisions and being responsible for them. There comes a time in life when Mom and Dad cannot tell you what is right and what is wrong. What happens in those tough times when there is no right and wrong — no black and white, just soft greys? Who tells you what to do? Which road ends up being not taken?

It was a warm Sunday morning with the African sun shining into the living room through the white netted curtains. We all sat on the couch staring at the news on television and nibbling on the idlis that Mom had made for breakfast. Usually on a Sunday morning we all would have so much to say — to fill in the rest of the family about our past week — but that day was different. There was just this eerie silence as we all sat lost in our thoughts. The following day was Monday, the seventh of May, the last day for me to either accept or decline the university offer from America.

This life-changing decision lay solely in my hands since my parents refused to influence me in any way. When I asked

Mom for her opinion, she simply shrugged and replied, 'It's your life at the end of the day, Meena!' 'Uh,' I thought, 'why can't such decisions be made for you?' But that's what growing up is all about! Tense, I sat on the edge of the couch as a pretty woman read the news, but I was not listening to what she was saying for my mind was elsewhere.

I looked at my younger sister sitting on the couch opposite. Who would I fight with if I left behind that little pest? If I left for America, how could I have pillow fights with my sister and with whom would I fight to sit in the front seat of the car? In America who would give me advice every five minutes? Who would set curfews for night parties? Who would cook me those delicious idlis? Who would proof-read my essays? I glanced at my little ginger cat and stroked her between her ears. Whose purring would put me to sleep at night? And then I looked out of the window at that warm and glowing African sun, the uncrowded mud roads, the mango trees in the garden, the noisy little African kids in the neighbourhood: this was home! How could I leave it? Was I ready to face that big bad world? I was content in my little bubble of comfort and happiness. Why spoil things?

But then I thought about my life's ambition. No universities in Zambia were of the calibre of American universities. And I wanted to study Public Health in a world-renowned university so that I could land an NGO job and then return to Zambia to serve the people here. I wanted to be the reason for the smiles on the faces of poor malnourished African children. I could not achieve this goal of mine with a standard Zambian education. I had to open my wings and learn to fly, to reach greater heights; after all, the sky was the limit!

At that moment, I made my decision. 'Daddy, I will go study in America! I will accept the university offer.' My Dad jumped up and hugged me. He did look a little sad but with a smile said, 'Go to the land of opportunities and make me proud!'

Two months later we all stood in a circle at the airport holding hands.

I tried my best to act all grown up and tough and wiped off the slight tear at the end of my eye. But then it was my mother who began to cry. She is a very strong woman never given to tears, but that day she cried.

Finally it was time to go and I waved goodbye from behind the red boundary line.

As the plane took off and rose above the ground, I watched what had been my home for the last sixteen years of my life grow smaller and smaller ... the cities, towns, villages, lush green plantations and savannah dry lands all became a miniscule dot that soon disappeared. I took a deep breath and knew then my new life had begun.

Meena Murugappan

Water Service

I travel a lot between Bengaluru and my native place Salem. The two cities are well connected by a nice day train. During one of those boring journeys, I had a pleasant experience.

When our train pulled into Dharmapuri station, four boys hopped in. They had no luggage but were carrying five water bottles each. I was surprised. This part of Tamil Nadu is known for its hot summers, but so many bottles of water were too much for them, I thought.

They could be selling bottled water, but they didn't look like hawkers. They were well dressed and looked like a bunch of school kids. After a few minutes, one of them approached me and asked 'Do you need drinking water Sir?'

My water bottle was almost empty. I nodded my head and opened my wallet to pay him. But he asked for my empty bottle.

'Why do you need it?' I asked puzzled, handing the bottle to him. He did not reply but opened the cap and poured water from one of his bottles into mine. Then he asked me for two rupees. Two rupees only? I couldn't contain my surprise.

Noticing my surprise, the boy said, 'Sir, we are not hawkers. In this station, the government has provided free, purified drinking water for the public. We fill this water in our bottles and refill it for the passengers. For this service we charge a nominal fee of two rupees. That's all!'

'But the passengers can refill their bottles themselves, can't they?' I asked.

'Of course, they can. But most of them are hesitant to get off the train. There are uncertainties like what if there is a long queue near the water tap? What if they can't find the water tap? What if the train leaves before they return? What if they fall down while gotting into a moving train? They worry about all these things and many times end up not leaving the comfort of their seats.

'By providing this service, we help them to make use of the public water facility instead of paying much more for bottled water. We fill our bottles before the trains come and charge only a fraction of what bottle water would normally cost.'

'Okay. But what do you do with the money?'

'We buy books.' I was pleasantly surprised as he continued, 'We are a group of four friends from poor families. Whenever a train comes, we provide this water service and collect our service charges. We save the money in a piggy bank and use it to buy our text books, notebooks and stationary.'

This incident occurred almost five years back. Those teenagers are probably in college now. I hope that their friendship continues and helps them take their entrepreneurial skills to the next level. After all it is true what they say: 'When good friends get together, they can take on the world!'

N. Chokkan

10

MEMORABLE MOMENTS

A memory is what is left when something happens and does not completely unhappen.

—Edward de Bono

After Twenty Years

It was a summer night in 1994. I stood on the terrace of my house with my dearest school friends, Abha and Suprit.

At the end of that summer, we would enter our last year of school. Already summer's charms had faded, for the humongous burden of the Board exams was upon us. Life was — wake up, study, bathe, breakfast, study, study, study, lunch, nap, study, chill for an hour, study, dine, study, go to sleep. Gone were the days of tramping through the woods, playing football and increasingly noticing girls (or boys)!

Was Abha my first crush? I don't know. There were many crushes those days, but the Board exams tended to make them fade away. But not Abha. She lived right across the street, right next to Suprit. We were in the same school, same class. She was tall, frail and fair with a face that would certainly light a thousand lamps. But most of all, she was intelligent.

It was the conversations that forged a bond between us. Three worried teenagers in a time when India was changing fast. The economy, politics, our futures, our parents' style of parenting, our freedom, our duties — we all had an opinion. There were fights, but perhaps the bond between us was so strong that it could not be broken. Little did we know that time would sunder them, so easily and effortlessly!

Suprit was my best friend and my rival when it came to grabbing the attention of girls. That was a race I'd lose easily — he was outgoing, charming, athletic and very entertaining. I was rather nerdy, bookish, too intellectual perhaps. But Suprit stuck by me, because we were such opposites. We complemented each other; he had much to learn from me, and I from him.

And so we come to that night when we all had met for a group study. There was much to cover — doubts in Physics and Mathematics (where I drew blank), on English and Biology (where I could hold forth). And as things went, the conversation drifted as usual.

India had just launched the Prithvi missile, and we were wondering what would happen next. Suprit said (or was it Abha?) that it may provoke a war, someone else retorted how it would be a deterrent; there was talk of an arms race and how the money would be far better spent on schools.

And then we began to discuss schools and the education system, how all teaching was mechanical and uninteresting. We veered on to graduation, our employment prospects and which jobs would fetch more money. Suprit was keen on joining the army (which he later did) and Abha and I were thinking of medicine. She is now a doctor; I've drifted along, a scientist once, now a copywriter and poet.

We had assembled after dinner supposedly to do our lessons, but it was the future that captivated us. It was perhaps 10 or 11 p.m. when we struck a deal that we remember even today, for the time of its fruition is coming near. We had studied O'Henry's *After Twenty Years* in our English paper; we decided to emulate the lesson.

We would meet each other twenty years from that date, and see where we had reached! Would we succeed? Or would our dreams congeal? Would we be able to meet at all? After twenty years, we decided we would meet at the same place, on the same date, and we swore on our teenage years!

The years passed, we left school and went our own ways. For some time we lost touch with each other. But as we moved into the twenty-first century, the internet, email, cell phones, and now the social media has helped us keep in touch. Suprit's in the army, and doing well. Abha is a doctor and married to her sweetheart. I am here, writing this article. But we still intend to keep our date.

Where there was fear there is knowledge, where there was hope there is truth, where there was innocence there is maturity. But where there was an intense friendship, there is still a vintage longing. And a few years from now, we three — in our thirties now — will meet one summer night, and fulfil the promise we made to each other long ago.

As Ratan Tata says, 'A promise is a promise.'

Raamesh Gowri Raghavan

It's a Girl Thing

Studying in a co-educational school has its perks. You don't stare dumbly at the opposite sex when they are trying to get through to you. You have a healthy sense of competition, both in the classroom and on the field; you grow up with them and see them become young men.

Imagine then after fifteen years of studying with boys, you end up in an all-girls college! Culture electrocution would be putting it mildly. True, it was one of the best colleges in the city; it was my choice to do the particular course and I fortunately had one of my closest friends from school, who would be my classmate in college as well. But nothing, absolutely nothing can prepare you for the shock when you enter a class full of fifty-odd girls in various states of girly-ness!

As my friend and I entered the class, we saw some girls were combing their hair, some touching up their lipsticks, some giggling away and a majority of them murmuring into their phones and blushing. Oh, and all of them were dressed up enough to think we actually studied in a co-ed college where boys would notice what we were wearing!

My friend and I felt like we were aliens in this setup; and we resigned ourselves to at least three years of nun-hood. That day, we had dressed in the first thing that came to our hands at the unearthly hour of 7 a.m. and had trudged in to class. As we got used to the college environment, we found ourselves a small group of friends who, like us, were anomalies to the estrogen-bubble that the others seemed to be in. Every morning, we would practically drag ourselves out of bed, somehow get ourselves into class, and only show signs of stirring as our names were called out during roll call.

Resigned to our fate, actually it turned out to be more fun than expected. We slowly got into the groove of things — lunch times used to be spent finishing off home-made dabbas quickly and rushing downstairs to the canteen to eat the yummy food they served. Invariably, one of the pretty girls in the gang was sent to do the payment and the food collection, since the guy behind the counter had a secret crush on her!

There is something so liberating about not caring what you are doing, how you look and just being yourself. Though we didn't know it while we were there, that's exactly how life was. It was the time when I learnt to gossip and be in a group without boys. During class, we would often be caught reading *Cosmopolitan* and be thrown out for disorderly behaviour, where we would continue our discussions in peace.

Another time, we decided to harass one of our most gullible teachers while two of us staged a fight, abuses et al and the poor thing didn't know what to do; all this, when the whole class was in on the joke.

There were teachers who commanded respect and no one tried to mess with them. But the hapless ones paid the price. Sure, we had our share of fights and hair-pulling episodes, but it was a novel experience ... being with a bunch of neurotic eighteen-somethings. As classmates grew closer, individual group traits would stand out — the backbenchers, the troublemakers (that was us), the desi 'kya-re' gang who were waiting for their Shah Rukhs to whisk them away, the studious MBA-after-this types, the best-friends-for-life types and finally the marriage-material types. And surprisingly, we did manage three years without any collateral damage to one another.

Years later, I'm in touch with my group of six friends, each of us caught up in our whirlwind lives. But we look back on those three years with the fondest of memories, probably the only time in our lives when we could actually be just us because ... no one cared about who was judging whom. There were no boys to impress and we were all queens in our own right.

Ranjani Rengarajan Deoras

Lost and Found

I consider her my 'first' friend. Right from our good old school days, she was the quieter one and I the naughtier one. She would never speak in front of strangers and in many ways I was her official spokesperson. And boys who tried to woo her mostly came to me. Even though her mother was my teacher, it did not affect our friendship. In between sharing tiffin boxes and notebooks, our world seemed complete. There were many in the school who admired our friendship and there were some who felt jealous for reasons known best to them.

When she was in high school, she lost her father and as the eldest child of the family, she rose to the occasion and I marvelled at the way she picked up the threads of her life with lots of grace and grit.

Before we could celebrate our eighteenth birthday together, we had to part ways as my father was transferred and we moved to a new city. She gave me a doll as a parting gift and we promised to be in touch through letters (those were the days when nobody in India had heard of mobile phones or unlimited talk time). We wrote long letters to each other sharing details about our lives. As she was the eldest child, under family pressure she had to get married early, even as we were pursuing our graduation course. I could not attend her marriage due to my exams.

The letters kept coming at regular intervals giving me details about her new life as a married woman. And through the same letters, I came to know about the birth of her son and daughter. The photographs gave me a glimpse of her new family members. We remained in touch for almost a decade through letters and then somehow we lost contact.

But then there were many occasions when I did think of her. And sometimes when my other friends talked of their 'first' friend, I always thought of her. I also thought of ways to dig out some information about her whereabouts. But then somehow it did not happen the way I desired. Years flew by but the memories remained.

On June 2010, one of my juniors in school got in touch with me on Facebook and thanks to her, I could finally manage to get my friend's mobile number . On a sultry evening, I called her up asking her where the hell she had been all these years. Our happiness knew no bounds as we chatted with each other, wondering whether it was the same voices we were hearing. I found out that she now resided in Goa and immediately we made plans to meet each other.

Finally in August 2010, I arrived in Goa. Before she came to the airport, she kept on asking, 'Will you recognise me?' We were meeting after twenty years, which is a long, long time indeed.

I was looking the other way when she came rushing towards me and as we hugged each other, school days felt so far yet so very near. For the next three days, we kept on talking and laughing squeezing in as much of the two decades as we could. Suddenly, we felt like teenagers again talking about those boys who gave us Amul chocolates and revelling in the taste of 'chatpati' (boiled chana garnished with onions, green chillies and tomatoes) that we used to have after school. Suddenly we rediscovered our teenage years in our adulthood. Age was certainly not a dirty word. Most importantly, we did not feel that we were meeting after twenty years. So many changes had crept into our lives, but somewhere, something had remained the same.

She was my guide in Goa and took me around from one beach to another. Every time I ventured far into the sea to enjoy the rolling waves, she would scream and call me back by my nickname. And suddenly amidst the sound of roaring waves, I felt a sense of deep affection when she called me by that name. With delicious prawn curry and chicken masala, my meals were a royal affair. When I expressed my desire to have gobi manchurian in a restaurant, she told me not to order it as her son really makes it well. And yes, in the evening I was treated to mouth-watering home-made gobi manchurian.

Three days ended too soon and as I hugged her to say good-bye at the airport, we knew this time we would not lose touch with each other. Meeting after twenty years also proved one thing: even though both of us have gained weight in the last two decades, the tight hug still feels the same — warm and loving.

Deepika

My Banjo

I was fourteen when I learnt to play the banjo. My music teacher, Mr Biswas, had been thrilled when I showed a keen interest in this beautiful instrument, and very soon I became his favourite student.

Back then, I was the only student in the school who had learnt how to play the banjo. My teacher taught me a number of tunes, ragas and also a lot of songs like 'Vande Mataram' and the national anthem. I practiced everyday and Mr Biswas was very happy with my efforts though the same could not be said about me.

In school, each festival or occasion was celebrated with a lot of enthusiasm, and so was Independence Day. There were endless march-past practices, long hours of singing rehearsals and the atmosphere was filled with the spirit of patriotism.

On the day of the flag-hoisting ceremony, while waiting for the chief guest, I saw a banjo placed near the stage. I smiled thinking Mr Biswas was going to give a performance and that it would be a rare treat.

Suddenly I heard my name being announced. 'Why are they calling me, am I going to be punished in front of everybody? Oh my God! Someone must have complained about me mimicking the Math teacher!' I thought in dismay.

Mr Biswas was waiting near the stage, an incomprehensible look on his face. 'Quickly, take your position,' he said.

'For what, Sir?'I asked bewildered.

'You have to play the national anthem on the banjo as soon as the flag is hoisted by the chief guest.'

I turned pale at the prospect and my knees felt like jelly. Was this an opportunity or a punishment?

'Who, me? I am not prepared Sir, I can't do this.' I stammered.Disregarding completely what I had said, he went on, 'Take your cue when you see the flowers falling from the flag. The Principal, is watching you. Best of luck!'

That was it! What about my shivering hands? How on earth had I landed myself in such a predicament?

While the chief guest made his speech I closed my eyes and recited the Gayatri mantra in my mind. When I opened my eyes and took a deep breath, I felt a lot more in control. As the tricolor was unfurled, I was overcome with a strange feeling of excitement. I started playing the national anthem, chest swelling with pride, and though I broke out in gooseflesh, I knew my performance was good. A beaming smile from Mr Biswas validated it beyond doubt.

It was Mr Biswas's confidence in me that reinforced my faith in the power of prayers. Even today after many years whenever I am on edge, I remember this incident while chanting my prayers and it never fails to give me the boost I need.

Arti Sonthalia

Stuff Dreams are Made of!

I was something of an anomaly in my teenage days. For one, the boys in my class were stunned that I could tell the leg side from the off side. The girls, on the other hand, thought it was strange that I did not hero-worship the cricketers, for that was the sole reason they even followed the game.

While I genuinely admired many cricketers, the man who stole my heart was not a cricketer. He was not even a celebrity in the ordinary sense of the word. The man I had the biggest crush on, in my teen years, was a cricket commentator. The man in question had receding hair and gaps between his teeth. While he certainly made me feel better about the gap between my own front teeth, he won my heart because he was so brilliantly articulate and wrote passionately about the game. He was probably one of the reasons why I chose to study Mass Communication in post-graduation, an idea that had formed in my mind when I was as young as fourteen. If there was any job worth doing, it had to be this, I had decided.

The prospect of travelling to exotic countries, talking and writing about cricket, even getting paid for it would send shivers of pleasure down my spine. Many a times I vividly dreamt and even role-played sharing the mike with him in a TV studio.

So, here I was, eighteen years old, a college student, firmly set on the path of becoming a journalist and still an enthusiastic cricket fan. There was a charity cricket match that was going to be played in my city but I did not have tickets for it. Luckily, at the last minute my friends offered me a ticket. I felt so lucky, because I knew that the match was going to be covered by my favourite commentator. This was something of a rare occurrence as his channel sadly did not have the rights to many of the matches that had been played in the past few years.

In the match, the first half went on unceremoniously. But for me, just the thrill of watching a cricket match live and the players in action was more than enough. During the break between the innings, I was extremely excited! One of the other sportscasters, a colleague of my hero, had come near my stand to interview one of the players! On seeing him, I ran close to the fence that separated the spectator stands from the playing arena and waved to him. Incidentally, he came close to the fence and started chatting with some spectators. Now, delirious and very keen that he should pass on my 'greetings' to my hero and let him know of my existence, I excitedly told him about how much my hero meant to me, and how his presence and writings drove my interests and ambitions.

He gave me a patient hearing and promised to pass on a hand written note to my hero. Then, he gave me quite a surprise! He leaned over and whispered to me that he just might be able to let me into the media box and introduce me too. I was ecstatic, I couldn't believe my ears! True, this was just a charity event and didn't have the usual security and crowd hassles that an international match would, but it was such a treat!

So, as per plan, I went over to the media box sometime before the match ended and was told to wait in a room. Then the sportscaster I had met earlier told me that he had a surprise for me! Could this evening get any better? It did! The sportscaster had realised my intense feelings for the commentator from our short conversation by the stands and had decided that I should be shot for a little segment with my hero for a special show on their channel. I was on cloud nine — to be on television with the man himself was something I had never really thought, it was beyond my dreams!

And then, I finally met him. After pinching myself several times to ensure that this was no dream, I shyly told him about how he was such a great role model. His modest demeanour and encouraging words only bowled me over some more.

During the show, when I confided to him that I was a little camera shy, he assured me that the camera was no monster and even if it was, I had no choice but to face it head on, if I was serious about becoming a journalist. Feeling reassured by his humour and comforting voice, I took my place in front of the camera with him. The rest of the shoot went great; I felt natural and spoke with ease. It just felt so right to be there.

By the end of it, I felt like a little kid let lose in a chocolate factory! I couldn't contain my excitement in meeting my star and being shot for a television show with him. The icing on the cake was my friends and family calling me up from all over the country, to tell me what a great job I had done and how I was an absolute natural on television.

I have always treasured this memory. It reminds me that no dream is too big. As for my hero, I'd like to thank him forever for making an impression in my adolescent mind, that it's important to follow your heart, and even more important, to be able to wake up every morning and feel happy about going to work, every single day. More importantly, I was thankful to him for being such a positive inspiration during those unsure teenage years, and finally, for being every bit of the role model I had ever thought him to be.

Hamsini Ravi

Transformed

After endless arguments with her parents she was finally getting married to her sweetheart. All she wanted was to live with him. People were still so old-fashioned, she thought. What was the big deal? Her friends were doing exactly what they felt. She had been the foolish one, telling her parents about it all. She should have just moved in with him. It would have been so cool. After all, she was nineteen and a half, and fully capable of taking decisions. All this jing-bang about nothing, she thought. Hall full of guests, drinks flowing, a band playing somewhere, when all she wanted was to be with him.

Someone called out to her. Her younger sister, all grown-up in a rose-coloured organza lehenga came to escort her to the mandap. There was a sparkle in her eyes, of tears or of happiness, she could not tell. But she knew that her sister would treasure this moment forever. So would she, she thought grudgingly, as she made her way through the flower-bedecked pathway amidst a hushed crowd of guests, with the strains of shehnai ushering her to the area where the ceremony was to be performed.

The glow of the fire was reflected on her face. She sat next to her beau, a bundle of nerves and with a fluttering heart. Her senses were in a state of alertness though they almost seemed to be a part of someone else. She hardly was aware of her limbs, for they obeyed orders not her own; her mind was dulled and her thoughts had volition of their own.

The shlokas and mantras made no sense to her, but she could feel their potency in her veins, as they infused a reverence and awe which she could not fathom. She looked askance at him, and was surprised to see him muttering whatever the priest would tell him and he seemed to be enjoying the whole process. Perhaps, he too was caught up in the spell of the moment. She would remember to tease him about it later. So much for all his modern ideas!

Suddenly, there was a lull, and she saw her father rise. The priest was asking her father to take her hand and place it in the hands of her husband to-be. She could feel the trembling of her father's fingers as he clasped her hand firmly, as if never to let go. She remembered the time when she was taken to pre-school as a toddler; on the first day her father had held her hands in the same way. That was a new phase of her life, and so was this, she thought, as her father carefully placed her hand in the hand of his son-in-law.

The seven times circling of the holy fire marked the end of the marriage ceremonies. She was now his wife. The gaiety in her sister was unmatched today, she thought, as she caught her eye and smiled. She saw her mother gazing at her, and went across and gave her a hug.

'Mamma, I'm tired,' she said.

'Of course, darling, go and lie down for a while. I'll get hot water for your feet and a change of clothes. Tomorrow will be another hectic day.'

She could discern a slight tremor in her mother's voice, as she wrapped a shawl around her.

Days after, as she sat looking at the album of her wedding photographs, she realised that she would cherish that day for it had brought so much happiness to those who cared for her. She saw the joy reflected in the eyes of her parents and sister. She saw herself in red and gold in various poses with her dashing husband. She saw the final wave of the hands when she left for her husband's home. She was living with her sweetheart just as she had dreamed of, but her home also had a place for her parents and sister, if they chose to visit her. She had opened the doors of her house for them.

Later, she would put little notes for each snapshot, she thought, to commemorate the events and perhaps tell her children about them one day.

Monika Pant

War Zone Super Hero

Mr India, save me! Mr India ... go get him! Get him!

Tring ... 'Wake up! The Matron is here! If you are not ready in fifteen minutes, you will have to stand outside the dining hall again!'

I hated being rudely woken up especially in the middle of my favourite super hero, Mr India dreams, and definitely not by Atul, who had the most shrilling, irritating, squirrel-like voice.

'... was always late for class ... didn't work ... was made to stand outside the class and got screamed at and played and played till the sun went down' — that sums up my fourteen years of boarding school experience, except for one vital part — the dormitory. The dorm was my domain; I had the topmost bunk near the window, and no one ever dared to set foot on my bed.

Atul wasn't exactly my buddy. He was someone I shielded when the seniors were out on a bullying spree. In return, he summarised chapters for me and saved me a seat in the dining hall. In fact, over the years, he did other little things for me whenever he got the chance.

It all happened the year the Gorkhaland movement gained

momentum. We had a month long holiday due to indefinite strikes. In those days, only two meals were served and there were no Sunday special treats as stocks were running dry. We were mostly confined to the school premises. The only good part was that we were allowed to take naps in the daytime as there was nothing better to do.

'Many bizarre things are happening outside, right now as we speak,' announced our Matron.

'Is there going to be a war?' asked a junior. 'Will bombs and missiles be the answer to the years of suppression amongst the kind and gentle hill people?'

'The group outside is screaming "Gorkhaland is all that we want,"' informed another who had managed to catch a glimpse of the road.

But all this did not really matter to me. I was preoccupied with greater things, like my upcoming birthday. I was turning fourteen. The seniors had said they looked forward to initiating me into their group and the juniors envied me. Atul said nothing as he had crossed this incredible milestone last week. This was one race that had been rigged, as he was lucky to have been born before me. I felt betrayed since I was the one who protected him and not the other way round! Solace came from the fact that there was nothing I could do about this. It was best forgotten as I resumed playing my 'strong man' role.

The next morning I was told that Atul and I were to accompany the Matron to the market. Both our birthdays had been rather uneventful, with no cake or presents as the shops remained mostly closed following directives from the local leaders. So as things seemed a bit relaxed, the Matron asked us to get ready for our treat.

We reached the market soon enough and Matron got busy. I decided to explore whereas Atul, being his usual obedient self, chose to stay put. I observed that people were happy and smiling, which was a rarity in those troubled times.

Suddenly, a tall, well-built man came running up the road pushing everyone out of his way. He was followed by another man. I wondered what was happening. Why were two grown up's racing each other in the middle of the marketplace? Could it be 'Sports Day' for grownups? I looked around for some colourful flags, but there were none. It couldn't have been a sports day. The crowds started dispersing quickly. I looked around for Matron and Atul but could not see them. An old man rushing past urged me to run and hide. That is when I witnessed the most shocking scene of my life.

The two men, who had been running till a moment back, were standing in the middle of the marketplace. They were now inching closer to each other. Then I saw it — it was a metal object; about the size of a ruler ... was it a knife? What was happening? Were they actually fighting? The only fight I had imagined was when Mr India beat up the goons. Who was the goon amongst these two? Was he going to kill the other man? I was scared. A strange silence of fear had gripped the marketplace as everybody looked on.

Suddenly I heard the familiar voice I hated. 'Noooooo!' It was a shrill squirrel-like voice. I saw a frail young boy run up to the man with the knife and say, 'Good afternoon, Sir. My name is Atul and I study in standard seven. Sir, please don't hurt this man. Isn't this land on which I am standing, all that you want? If you let go of this man, I will also go away from here. I promise I'll make my father take me away from this school and never come back here. So do we then have a deal, Sir?' The man looked ferociously at Atul and then turned around and walked away. There was a huge murmur of relief from the watching crowd.

As I stood there speechless, shivering from the cold fear emanating from within, I saw a brave heart rise to the occasion to save a life. This was not a dream. That day I saw a real-life teenage super hero.

Arjun K. Bose

11

IT'S NEVER TOO LATE

You may be disappointed if you fail, but you are doomed if you don't try.

–Beverly Sills

Friends Forever

It was 31st of July, Founder's Day, at my old school.

It had been exactly three months since I had given my board exams and had started studying at my new school in Chandigarh. I had hated the whole idea of leaving my hostel friends and going back to Chandigarh, but Mom and Dad had been missing me. I was their only child and I had been studying in Mussourie for nine years. I had reluctantly agreed to their decision, on the condition that they let me visit my friends whenever we had a big occasion in school. So here I was, on my way to Mussourie, smiling to myself at the thought of meeting Michelle, my best friend.

Michelle and I had been friends ever since the day she had joined school in the fifth grade. We had the same interests — our taste in music, books, food, clothing were just the same. Just by looking at each other we knew what the other was thinking. Everyone in school knew that if there was something that required team work, it was for certain that we would be partners. When we played basketball, we two would be enough for the opponents. We had a rhythm that made others jealous. We had decided that after passing out from school, we would go to a finishing school in Switzerland and then study literature. It all seemed so well planned.

I had remembered to get a box of sweets for Ram Charan, our gate man. He was happy to receive it and opened the gates for our car to drive in. As usual, I was engulfed by the beauty of the school, its location amidst the mountains. The scent of the trees mesmerised me, it reminded me of the years I had spent running, walking, laughing, crying and just simply staring at the scenic beauty. After meeting the Principal, I headed straight for Michelle's dormitory, on the way meeting or rather screaming with joy and hugging every person I knew.

Michelle was not in her dorm, where could she be? It was already six o clock, she should have been here for a change of clothes. While waiting for her I met other friends, but my heart was longing to see her. Finally she came — I jumped with joy and gave her a big hug. I couldn't wait to tell her and hear all that had been happening in her life. She seemed a little lost; at first I thought it was the shock of seeing me that made her speechless, but slowly, it got unbearable. I demanded that she tell me what was on her mind. She shrugged it off, saying that it was the practices for Founder's Day that was getting her too tired.

After dinner we headed for the practice rooms, where I watched the entire class perform. It was lovely to be in the same ambience again. I felt a part of everything, even though I was not involved. But I was not a part of what I had come for — Michelle looked distant and aloof. She was so involved with her new set of friends that she was unaware of me. I tried holding her hand and getting her to talk, but she wanted to get away. This had never happened before; she was a new Michelle, not the one I had travelled for!

Things had changed. The phrase 'friends forever' had lost its meaning for me. I knew she had moved on, but I was still attached to her. I had bought a wooden carved wall hanging for her with both our names engraved on it, but I didn't want to give it to her. Anger took over the pain, I wanted to go home and cry. I felt I had lost control over my emotions; I felt I betrayed and hurt. Next day, before the evening function was to begin, I packed my bags. I wanted to leave before the show. I wrote a note to Michelle which went like this;

Dear Michelle,

'Friends forever' was what we had promised to be to each other in all the beautiful years we had spent together, but I never realised we would lose our way. It would be a lie if I told you that I was glad you have found new friends. I had wanted you to be there just for me, but had not realised life goes on; we cannot hang on to the same branch forever. All the time I have spent with you remains fresh in my mind, I shall keep them with me 'FOREVER'. You have been special to me and have been a part of me and I will always remember the sweet memories, the sour ones shall pass away.

Love forever,

Ayesha

The next time I met Michelle was during our school reunion, which was being held after ten years. She walked up to me and hugged me. She looked at me with pain in her eyes, as though she needed me and had missed me. I immediately understood that this was her way of apologising. The years of togetherness had made us reconnect with each other.

She had the note I had written in her hand; we both read it together and laughed. We finally became 'friends forever'. My sixth sense told me that a new chapter of our friendship was going to begin and this time it was going to remain for a long time. The reunion had actually been a 'reunion' of two friends.

Arti Sonthalia

From Kavita

'There is only one success: to be able to spend your life the way you wish.'

When I was in school, I was an introvert and extremely shy. I couldn't make friends with the ease the way others did. When I changed my school, I thought I would be lonely in the new school, but on the first day itself, Kavita confronted me. She was beautiful, confident and very intelligent. She introduced me to her friends and to my surprise, I fitted in well with everybody like a required piece in a jigsaw puzzle.

One day, I asked her, 'What made you come up to me that first day and make me your friend?' She became pale and the glow in her eyes dimmed. She said, 'I didn't want you to suffer in the manner I did. I know how horrible it is when you don't have anybody to talk to you or care for you.' I was bewildered. 'How did you overcome it?' I asked.

'I too, like you, was a reserved person. Moreover, I loved to study, but was too weak a person to share my views with others. I was a naive and vain human being. I lost all my friends, gradually I began to lose interest in academics, I no longer had any faith in myself or in God, my dreams were collapsing and I couldn't do anything.' Here she stopped, sighed and smiled and then continued, 'But every cloud has a silver lining and there is light at the end of every dark tunnel. I met with an accident. As I lay on the street, gasping and praying with every breath, I realised that I still wanted to live. I begged God to give me one chance, to give me one ray of hope and I would enlighten my whole world with it.

'I was in the hospital, the pain in my head was excruciating, my mother had to give me two bottles of blood and when I opened my eyes, I had turned over a new leaf. I had faith in God, and decided to gain everything I had lost. I was no longer afraid of losing anything more; I had just defeated death, now nothing was more important to me than my life. I knew I could change my fate no matter what it takes.'

From Kavita I learnt that even if the whole world turns its back on you, just keep one thing in mind — you are not isolated because the person who is isolated is not the one who has lost relatives or friends, but the one who has lost himself.

Kavya Lakhani

Identity Crisis

When I look into the mirror,
I see ...
Everything including the darkness
that hides within me.

I wonder if it is true,
The picture
Of myself which I drew.

Am I still myself?
Am I what I want to be,
Or just a photocopy
Of what people want to see!

Maybe I have lost my identity
I have forgotten who I actually am
But people tell me, as long as one's cool
One shouldn't care a damn!

Sometimes I wonder ... maybe it is time
to go up to the divine,
But I stop myself as I relieve the pain,
in dying to fill myself again.

As I look up into the sky
I wonder how much more I must try
Before I remove every obstacle, every thought
Of the misconception of who I am.

Enough of jumping in the lake
Enough of breathing lows of the state,
It is time to be myself,
Enough of being fake.

I don't care if I drop my scores
I don't care if they shut their doors
I don't care if they ask for a fee
As long as they know I am ... just me.

I just want to be me
Not perfect at all
Just perfectly me ...
It's time to move away from the mirror
It's time I let everyone know forever
That I am not who they think me to be
I am just ... me.

Now I am sure ... next time
When I look into the mirror
I'll see ...
Everything including the darkness
Moving away from me.

Rajeev Goenka

It's Never Too Late to Make a Friend

It was the annual Open Fete at school. I was with my group of friends. We had planned to make this last fete in our school life the most memorable one ever. I was in class tenth and knew that next year my close group of friends would not be any more together in the same school. Suddenly, I remembered the very same occasion in the previous year.

That day Sonakshi was walking alone in the school fete. Struck by her woe-begone air, I watched her going from stall to stall. Did she have no friends? But I knew the answer to that. She had none. She had joined my class that very year and had tried hard to adjust. But we all had our own groups and gangs in class. Quite water-tight! No one could enter, unless initiated by a member belonging to the particular group or one had the skill of cracking witty jokes.

'Hey! What are you looking at?' said one of my friends. 'Let's have some of those delicious veg kababs!'

'Listen,' I said, 'Why can't we call Sonakshi? She looks lonely.'

'Who?' said my friends in a chorus, 'That snooty girl? Why should we?'

'Anyway, she's with her kid sister.'

I turned and looked. Yes, her sister had joined her, and

hand in hand they walked through the fete, sampling the fare at each stall. Yet, when I passed her on the way to the pakoda stall, I could see the unmistakable glint of unshed tears as her eyes met mine, before she turned away.

That was a day I will never forget. I will always regret that I did not call her into my group. In fact, right through the one year that she was in my class, I had not befriended her. I did not realise that to be without a friend during high school was an awful situation to be in. She was unable to bear the fact that she had no friend to accompany her on school trips, none to share her triumphs with, no one to confide her longings in. How awful she must have felt!

I did not realise it then, but she left at the end of class nine, knowing well that she would have to repeat the class in another school. I wondered how she would have convinced her parents. Or had they really needed convincing? On the day she left, on a sudden impulse, I ran to her and asked her for an email address. She hesitated for a second and then gave it to me. Though it was too late to make amends as she was already leaving school, I intended to keep in touch.

Today, she has become my friend. Though we are no more in the same school, sometimes I send her an email and on rare occasions even chat online. We have discovered a mutual interest in Hollywood classics and we are also fond of the same books. I now understood that it is difficult to know how to behave in a new environment and so easy to make judgements about people. But there is one thing I can say without doubt, she is my only friend who will not receive exasperated words from me for forgetting my birthday.

Sadhika Pant

Mommy's Little Girl

Till today I have never come across a more striking looking fourteen-year-old. She was new in our school and even in an all-girl's school, she made heads turn. Her family had recently moved this side of town and she came across as a stuck-up south Bombay kid. Since she and I were the tallest in class, we had to sit together. Over the next couple of days I figured that she wasn't stuck up, just shy.

Gradually S and I became friends. She definitely came from a privileged family and had very liberal parents. Studies were not a priority. She missed school if she had been up watching movies all night with her cousins, and went on vacations abroad and shopped at the toniest stores in town.

I spoke about her so often that my family and friends in the building also wanted to meet her. The boys in my building were drooling for days after they saw her; my mother remarked that she was too mature for someone her age. As we became closer I started going to her place and was very impressed. She had a walk-in wardrobe. Her parents were never home so we could play loud music and talk on the phone for hours — privileges that were hard to come by in our homes. She failed in the unit tests but did not seem too concerned. I found that really strange and asked how her mother had reacted; she laughed sarcastically and let it pass.

The detective in me was intrigued and I started on my fact-finding mission. One day I dropped in unannounced at her place. Her dad was happy and said he had heard so much about me but S seemed fidgety and said I should not have dropped in just like that, her mom did not like it. I pretended like it didn't bother me, and said I would meet aunty today. She said her mom had to be called by her name, no one called her 'aunty'. Her mom breezed into the room just then and I instantly knew what was S's problem — her mom was gorgeous and even S would feel like a waif before her. Thank God for my round, bespectacled mom!

When she realised I was a tough cookie that was not likely to get intimidated by her, her mom tried to get friendly with me. Sure she wanted to be addressed by name and went on to tell me how S had signed up for aerobic classes and had to be prepared for the beach holiday. This was absurd; my folks only told me to prepare for exams. She gave me some spiel on how she had got married at sixteen and had S when she was eighteen so they were growing up together!

When I told my mother the entire saga, she said clearly the woman had a complex and was competing with her own daughter. Gradually S began confiding in me. She cried as she yearned for a normal mother who cooked and attended PTA meetings. She wanted a mother, not a pal who shared her clothes.

While she got oodles of male attention she steadfastly maintained that she would never date anyone. I asked her candidly if she feared that the guy would fall for her mom once he saw her? She smiled sadly and said no, because she would soon get married to whoever her dad chose for her. That evening I thanked my parents for who they were. I was allowed to play basketball without worrying about whether I would get dark. I could enjoy eating cake and not worry about an inch I may gain.

I decided S was the 'poor little rich girl' who needed help. When all of us made a plan from school to go watch a film, her mom decided she would come along. She came and everyone was floored. She paid for everything but S and I sulked. Later she asked the two of us to come for a drive with her. I mustered all the courage and decided to tell her off, even if it meant that she wouldn't let S talk to me ever again. Holding back my tears, despite S pleading with me, I declared that she was cruel and asked why was she ruining her daughter's life. Trust me to be dramatic even at that age! She looked shell shocked and asked me what I was talking about.

S was her mommy's little baby she insisted and would never have a problem with what mommy did. She said their family was different and that S would be married by eighteen. 'To live in a golden cage like yours?' I asked. Floodgates opened and for the first time I think mother and daughter spoke. Amidst tears, accusations, hugs and hostilities a lot was said and understood. Before dropping me home both of them thanked me and I called S's mom 'aunty' from then onwards!

Shifa Maitra

Pizza Hut

One Saturday morning, my friends, Xyna and Teena decided to go shopping. Shopping did not fascinate me, but on the agreement that I would stay in Landmark and browse through books while they shopped elsewhere in the mall, I decided to go along. Teena promised to treat us to lunch after that. At the mall, as promised, I was allowed to revel in the glorious collection of books while they marched off purposefully to the clothes shops. I spent a blissful three hours reading and drowning myself in the books on the store's shelves. By 2 o' clock, the two triumphant shoppers returned and announced that lunch would be at Pizza Hut.

Once there, we did not wait to be shown to a table but marched over to the first vacant table and settled ourselves amongst the shopping bags. We called out to the waiter who rushed from the adjacent table and took our order. Soon our pizzas were set before us and we dug in. We were hungry. Food, glorious food! As we ate, we talked about our hostel, the unfair rules that prevailed, the annoying people there (read seniors; we were first-year students) and so on. Once our meal was over, the bill arrived: Rs 725. Teena pulled out her credit card and put it inside the folder. The waiter took the card inside to process it. He returned promptly, but only to inform us that the card was not working. Teena had used the card just an hour back and it had worked fine. Could he please try again? He obliged us, but with the same result.

We looked into our purses and found that between the three of us we had only two hundred and fifty rupees. Xyna started clowning around and I laughed uncontrollably. We did not know what to do. Teena was very embarrassed and snapped at us. Xyna announced to everybody that Pizza Hut charged a heavy tax. She obviously did not know what she was doing and only added to the hysteria. Such fools we were — stuck in a restaurant with a huge bill and no money, and instead of thinking of a solution, we were giggling.

It was a serious situation. We decided to calm down and call our seniors (the same ones we talked about over lunch) and ask for money. Shocked as they were, they managed to round up seven hundred and fifty rupees and send it across through common friends (people are always short on cash in hostels). Coming up with a sum of rupees seven hundred and fifty in about fifteen minutes on a weekend when there is hardly anyone in the hostel was definitely not easy.

We paid the bill and walked back to our hostel, wondering what we would tell our seniors. Once there, as expected, we were met by the firing squad — our seniors, who gave us a piece of their mind about managing and using money wisely.

For all our grumbling, we knew that we were lucky we had them for friends, not just because they helped us out of a tight spot, but also because they cared enough to be furious with us about our foolish behaviour and then laugh over it with us.

Today, seniors and juniors do not get off on a great start most of the times because the issue of ragging hangs like an ominous shadow over them. If only the seniors could befriend their juniors without resorting to intimidation and earn their respect, college years could become as wonderful as it were for us!

Ashita Chandran

12

ON WISDOM

*Y*ou learn something every day if you pay attention.

–Ray LeBlond

Blending In

It doesn't matter if you are a teen or an adult, so let me ask you this — do you know the Sorting Hat in Harry Potter books? The one that decides the house categorisation of new students? It's not all fiction. There *is* a sorting hat ceremony that happens in real life all over the world, in companies, homes, and schools. In schools, it is especially hard because you don't have a second chance at all.

Normally, in India, students 'change'schools during their seventh, ninth or eleventh standards. I too joined a new school when I was thirteen, one that was known to be very strict (even the strictest school has its share of rule-benders!). Till then, I had studied only in all-girls school. This was the first time I was in a co-education school. On the third day of the school, I was asked if I had done my homework. I had not. There was a collective swivel as a particular section turned towards me and noted the fact. It looked as if the first-benchers had decided: I was not to be included in their gang.

The next day, I casually answered a question posed by a boy, and started discussing a book with him. I was finally delighted to talk about my favorite topic — story books! I was the only girl in my neighbourhood and all my best friends were boys. I did not realise that speaking with a boy labels you as 'that girl who speaks with boys'. Another bunch — the nerdy puritans, heirs of dharampatnis who consider boys as Satan's weapons — made their decision never to let me in.

This incident took place after two weeks. There is a mini-manhole near the lab building, which is filled with dirt. My library book accidentally fell into it. Without hesitation, I dived in and picked it up. I loved books! And my childhood was spent playing in mud with boys ... what's a little mud going to do when you live in a concrete jungle like Chennai?

In an ideal world (ruled by Disney), this would have made me the queen of the kingdom (that is, my school) but reality is obviously different. My peers were appalled at someone who was nuts enough to dive into the resident swamp to save a mere book. The teachers thought I was being a drama queen and gave a fair-sized dressing down, in front of every one. Now, the remaining girls in my class promised themselves they would never get entangled with a certified nutcase like me.

And the biggest irony of all was the boys! Now I was not a first bencher; I spoke to them with a sincere smile but I jumped into man-holes, so, naturally, I was too weird to be a friend and too tomboyish to pursue as a crush. So no one to befriend there too — in any case, boys of that age can never be friends with girls! So I ended up as a loner, always trying to fit in, acting as the joker because I only fit that description. And the other roles were already taken in any case!

The story does not end here. Though I did not have friends

at all in the first few weeks, one day I found myself being smiled at by a beautiful girl — one of the 'in'crowd. You see, every co-ed class has one or two 'sensational bombs' — pretty, flirty girls who talk to boys. Since they also find themselves alone, all of them become one collective 'gang' and hang out during recess and after school. It was one such beauty who had smiled at me.

I remember being stunned. And even a little scared, though I smiled back, and just like that, I became one of them. Indeed, with my thick spectacles and my buck teeth, I was completely out of place in that crowd, but they did not mind — they just needed someone who did not judge them, who could be their confidante. And plain, non-threatening me fit the description to the T, so they adopted me. They gave me friendship and they taught me how to survive when you don't fit anywhere.

And what was my role in their crowd? I listened, comforted, wiped their tears and cheered when they were ecstatic. I was a sponge to all their anguish, priorities, anger, and hopes. I was learning about unconditional acceptance. I was learning about proposing and rejecting. I was learning about hormones, the emotional gap between a girl and her parents, about lies and pretensions and how easy it is to be false and how difficult it is to be honest. I was learning about life.

They too gave me a lot, though some would debate it. The afore-mentioned female first benchers and puritans would wound me with a nasty look or line, but they shut up the minute I befriended this bunch. Coming from a middle-class family where girls call other men as anna (brother), I was clueless about talking to my male classmates, and in answering tricky questions ('Why is your skirt so tight') with frank answers ('The tailor lost a major bit of the cloth').

My new friends then took me under their wing and educated me about boys — how you never ever give them the opportunity to mock you or joke about you. When I went through my share of infatuations, they were there to give advice, caution and hold my hand.

This small crowd — known as the most notorious and good-for-nothing girls — were my teachers, guides, gurus who gave me lessons that I'd later use in my life. Thanks to them, I grew up to be compassionate with those who make mistakes, who have erred and suffered and learnt to go forward without regrets. I learnt never to gossip and never to let a secret escape my mouth. I learnt about human fallacy and that not everybody walks straight, and it's the ones who walk crooked who need the most understanding.

Yes, I did not complete school with the best grades or best compliments, but I know it was the best experience, for the seed to my future career as a children's writer was sowed right there, when I learnt to listen to the other side (isn't a teen just an overgrown and confused child, hoping to be loved and held by someone?). I think it is because of this that I do not have one best friend — I have many, who tell me everything about their life, without fear, guilt or terror. Wherever I go, I have strangers talking to me about their past indiscretions. I have met shopkeepers, boutique owners and saleswomen who share their innermost thoughts during our first and probably only meetings.

All through this, I understand what people want — acceptance and understanding, forgiveness and friendship from others. I give that, and find happiness. And I try to bring that wisdom in my writing, which is challenging and at the same time, enlightening. My teen friends, if you ever find yourself dealt a harsh blow by your school's Sorting Hat, do not despair — you *will* find friends, and they *will* impact your life to a great extent. Somewhere, somehow, your life will glean its wisdom from these years.

Radhika Meganathan

Defined by Numbers

It is that time of the year again, that time in May when the heat was killing, the time when many suicide prevention organisations start advertising, and when many nervous teenagers, with their palms sweating and hearts racing, sit in front of the computer waiting for their exam results.

Board exams — the one public exam that could determine your academic potential and your college admissions. Your future depends on the marks you score. Just one exam, yet it has the power to change everything, to define you.

I stared at the computer, blinking rapidly at the digital clock at the bottom. It wasn't time yet; fifteen minutes were still left for the results to be announced. Yet relatives had already started calling; my aunt from Mumbai, and my grandmother, who had already called twice, to find out what the verdict was. I swallowed and discovered I was feeling nauseous. Why should one exam being made into such a big deal, what about other exams you have taken? As I anxiously waited, my mind did a quick run of the examinations — I thought English had gone alright, but I did mess up those three sums in Math ....

'Anisha, have they come yet?' Mom called from the

bedroom, in a concerned voice. This was the longest half-an-hour of my life I thought. Before I could reply to her the digits of the clock changed and the moment had finally arrived.

The results were out! Names of the toppers were being announced on all the news channels (I knew I would never have been one of them), and with shaking fingers I typed my index number on the web site. I felt slightly dizzy as I scanned my marks; I reached for the calculator to work out my average. As I punched in the numbers and hit the equal button, I was horrified at the number that appeared — sixty-four. Sixty-four? Had I really done that bad? All that studying … and that's all I got? A sixty-four wasn't good enough. Not for my parents, for colleges, or even for me. Was that really all I could have scored? Was I that terrible a student? I had studied hard keeping in mind the long list of excellent colleges I'd been planning on applying to, all over the country. Every single one of them had cut-off marks. With my percentage they wouldn't even bother to look at my application. My aunt, my grandmother and everyone else would be so disappointed when they heard. 'What happened to Anisha?' they would think. Her brother had done so well, and all her cousins had graduated from such fine colleges!

I was vaguely aware of my mother coming to look over my shoulder. I heard her moan in disappointment. I heard my grandmother and aunt discussing that I was the first in the family to score such low marks and how it was time I started taking things seriously. My parents had not come right out and yelled at me, but they were clearly upset.

Most of my friends had been sympathetic, some were secretly pleased because I had done better than them in the preliminary exams, but all of them had found a hot topic for gossip.

Disappointment surrounded me from all sides. I had let down my whole family, and of course, myself. My marksheet just proved that I wasn't as good as my friends or my brother or cousins.

Later that night, I sat on my bed feeling miserable. I wondered if that feeling of being a failure would ever go. I lay back and shut my eyes, letting my mind travel to the time before I'd felt this feeling of worthlessness. I remembered the time when my brother and I were stuck alone in a car and had hopelessly lost our way. My brother could not make head or tail of the map we had with us but I'd managed to read it and bring us back safely. My parents had been overjoyed and congratulated me. Then there was that time when my friend had wanted to learn some dance moves and I had patiently taught them to her till she perfected them.

I thought of how one of my class teachers described me as an 'eloquent speaker' in my report card, or the countless number of times when people had referred to me as 'good friend', 'cheerful' or 'observant'. As I recalled all this, I realised that I was still all of those things; I was still that girl who had a sharp memory, read geographical maps well and was always willing to help. No matter what happened, there would always be some things that only I had and that only I could do. I was as good as anybody else or maybe in some matters even better.

Who said two small numbers can sum up who you are?

Niyantri Ravindran

Fathers Versus Sons

I was ready to take strike. My friend Sadiq shouted from the dugout, 'Karthik, only six balls to go and we need ten runs to win this match. Buddy, everything is in your hands!' Nine wickets had fallen. We had to win this exciting 'Fathers versus Sons' one-day cricket match.

One Sunday morning after practice, we sat and reviewed our performance as a team. We had challenged most of the teams in our locality and won against them, but we needed to play more practice matches. That is when Arvind came up with this wonderful idea — he suggested we play a 'Fathers versus Sons' cricket match. All of us agreed instantly.

That evening, we all tried to convince our respective dads. The dads discussed it among themselves and eventually agreed to play with us the following Sunday. It was 'a ten overs a side' match. All fathers and sons were suitably attired for the game with sports shoes and caps. Our respective moms and siblings were the spectators, watching us from the balconies.

We won the toss and elected to field. In the first over, we secured two wickets. We celebrated like we had won the match. But soon after, the Fathers' team gave an electrifying performance. We tried our best pace bowlers, but failed to contain them. In every over, they hit a few boundaries. The score board moved rapidly. It was baffling. We had thought that since they were much older, they would not be comfortable running between the wickets. They weren't, but to compensate for that, they used the velocity of the ball bowled at them and hit it for sixes and fours.

It was time to change the strategy. We brought in spin attack. But the thrashing continued. Finally, after the stipulated ten overs, they had scored one hundred and five runs.

After the thirty minutes refreshment break, our team came in to bat. The Fathers sent spin bowlers instead of launching a pace attack as they were not comfortable with too much running. We had never paid much heed to spin bowling and in no time our middle order collapsed. Scoring even a hundred runs seemed impossible. Fortunately, the tail-enders played amazingly well and managed to score some runs. We had some managed to pile up ninety-six runs in nine overs with nine wickets down. Now we needed ten runs in six balls.

I was at the batting crease with Sumeet at the non-striker's end. All the moms, brothers and sisters were clapping and cheering as Srinivas uncle took his run up. In the first ball I attempted a six, but the ball hit the edge of the bat and went in the other direction. It was a single. In the second delivery, Sumeet found a gap and we scored two runs. Sumeet retained the strike. In the third ball, a nervous Sumeet attempted a six, but failed. It was a single again. Everybody applauded our hundred. It was a relief.

We now needed to score six runs in three balls. The fourth delivery was bowled by Srinivas uncle. I swung my bat with all the power I had and the ball flew towards the boundary. Plump Gopi uncle was chasing the ball so we had the chance to go for three runs. But Gopi uncle was surprisingly fast. He fielded brilliantly and hurled the ball at the wickets. I fumbled just a few metres before reaching the crease and Gopi uncle's powerful and accurate throw hit the stumps. I was declared out. Our team was all out for one hundred and two runs. It was unbelievable … we had lost the match!

Our fathers celebrated their victory and the mothers clapped for them, while in our camp, we were busy blaming each other. Our heads hung in shame as the Fathers' team came to shake hands with us. Sensing our disappointment, they cheered us up and commended our efforts. They took us to a restaurant for lunch. Our moods had lightened by then and we were full of questions.'How could Gopi uncle run so fast and throw the ball exactly at the stumps?' I asked in amazement. Gopi uncle replied sportingly, 'Appearances are deceptive. Never underestimate a person by his looks!'

'You lost two of your best batsmen in the first over itself, but you still succeeded in piling up one hundred and five runs. How did you do it?'Ravi enquired. Srinivas uncle answered calmly, 'You should never lose hope, never give up and always keep your cool. Tough times do not last, but tough people last long. Never let success go to your head and failure to your heart.'

That is exactly what had happened with us. We were a powerful team that had not lost a match in the last one month. But today, because of our over confidence, we had lost to forty- and fifty-year-olds.

This was one of the best matches of our lives, which helped us learn some valuable lessons and strengthened the bond between friends, fathers and sons.

T.S. Karthik

Friend + Enemy = Frienemy

Every time I read articles on friends, there would always be one word I never really understood — Frienemy. But my oblivion to the meaning of the word didn't last long, because one day, a frienemy literally walked into my life.

Malvika and I became friends when we were twelve. We were in the same class in school, went for tennis together and seemed to be alike in almost every way. Our choice of music and books was uncannily similar. She was also the only one in my class who could keep up with my fast growing vocabulary of 'bad' words, which qualified her as one of my friends.

I remember once telling my mother that the reason we got along well was because she did not compete with me. I was a good student and my grades were always enviable. On the other hand, Malvika never scored well. Yet, she never nurtured feelings of envy. She accepted her grades and did not ever compete with me. At least that is what I thought in the beginning.

As we stepped into the dangerous teen years, our friendship was put to the test. We joined advanced classes for mathematics. That is when I noticed a change in her attitude, every time she solved a sum that I couldn't, she would smirk with pleasure, and not getting a sum that I did, would upset her.

This approach was replicated in the tennis court too. Her annoyance was obvious every time I won a match. Whenever the two of us hung out with another friend or went for camps, she would always try turning the others against me and isolate me. It is not difficult for a thirteen-year-old to figure out that this was not really how a friend was supposed to act.

In the ninth grade, the animosity between us was at its peak. But by then, I had learnt how to deal with it. I believed it was essential to be on good terms with her, because I had to spend eight hours every week with her in Math class and travelling by car-pool. Our friendship had been reduced to polite words and formal conversations.

It was an absurd friendship and superficial friendship. People were surprised when they learnt that we actually were at loggerheads with each other, rather than like 'BFF' (Best Friends Forever).

Gore Vidal said, 'Whenever a friend succeeds, a little something in me dies.' This is the psychology of a frienemy—a person who will appear as one of your really good friends, but from the inside, they are constantly planning ways to pull you down. But I've learnt to deal with it maturely. I know exactly which conversations are dangerous to tread upon. When Malvika says something patronising, I do feel bad, but I don't bite back.

It is up to us to realise that what such 'friends' say doesn't really matter. There is simply too much to do in our youth; after all we aren't here to please anyone — we just have to be what we are.

Shivani Singh

Hallmark of a Teenage Champ

'While we teach our teenage child all about life, our teenage child teaches us what life is all about.'

–Unknown

My son Debayan had just stepped into his teens when my wife and I decided to hone his chess talents. My wife waited long hours, as my son sparred with reputed players and coaches at the Gorky Sadan Chess Learning Centre in Kolkata.

Sometimes, the practice session would last as long as five hours; and though it did test my wife's patience, she always came out with a radiant smile. Kudos also to my thirteen-year-old, who was an epitome of patience, determination and grit. He never faltered at the marathon hours of rigorous training he had to undergo.

After a year, Debayan was confident enough that he could battle with the chess stalwarts and he desired to participate in the Telegraph FIDE rated Schools International Tournament, the premier chess tournament of our country.

Both my wife and I assumed that our son would be crushed by the far superior players in the championship and it would be a stumbling block to his new-found teen confidence. So, in good humour, we advised him to play the tournament only for fun and gain some valuable experience.

Our son surprised us by his seriousness as he played each game on its own merit. Not only did he display outstanding dedication, but also unflagging determination as he romped home against the best school kids of the sub-continent. On the penultimate round, he was pitted against one of the top-ranked participants who was a seasoned player at this high level of the game. No one, not even the most optimistic of coaches, gave Debayan much of a chance.

We waited in the adjacent hall, as our son's match got underway. His progress was conveyed to us by young chess observers, from time to time.

Debayan began on a sedate note and he steadily inched his way to an advantageous position. He could have held his rival to a draw and won honours but he decided to take a risk and attempt a win. He transformed his game to an attacking one. My wife bit her fingernails while a beaming chess analyst whispered to us that Debayan was sensing victory. He played with tenacity, courage and cool and had stretched his senior competitor. We were swamped with loud cheers from the playing arena as Debayan did us proud by overcoming his opponent and carving out a thumping victory.

As he walked out of the hall, he did not display and emotions, not even a dash of excitement as the reporters from national television channels, the newspapers and teens magazines thronged him for interviews.

When his mother congratulated him and I patted him on his shoulders, he remained cool as a cucumber. When I reprimanded him for taking an undue risk when he could have easily settled for a draw, he told me that he relished taking challenges in life and did not mind losing after a tough fight. He told us that only cowards run away from the scene of the battlefield. After the prize ceremony, Debayan seemed extremely delighted to receive his first cash award. He insisted we take him to a jewellery shop. Even before we realised what he intended to do, he had chosen a gold pendant and a chain for his mother. Believe me, Debayan spent almost his entire maiden prize money on the gift for his mother.

There were tears of joy not only in her eyes but also mine. What a glorious tribute from a son, a teen champ!

It saddens me to think how often we parents accuse teenagers of their rebellious attitude. How much we detest their ways of life, their attitude, their 'warped' mindset and their changing personalities. We forget that teenagers have minds of their own, we underplay their maturity, we overlook their genuine feelings — the deep love and tender affection that they silently hold for their parents. It is only those parents who devote time not money, shower their love, not kisses and hugs; and show that they really care often get back return gifts from their teenage children.

Debashish Majumdar

Home is Where the Heart Is

Five years is a long time. You grow five inches taller, add five more candles to your birthday cake, or worse still, outgrow the whole birthday affair.

In my case, five years means the time when I left five important things in my life — family, friends, house, food and freedom. I know it is puzzling. Leaving home should spell freedom, right? I thought so too when I first shifted to a hostel in 1998. But on day one, I was given a small slip with my admission form which had something obnoxious called 'Rules of the hostel'.

It read — 'Under no circumstances would you be allowed to stay out of the hostel past 6 p.m.' I gasped, but being a hopeless optimist, I thought that with time, the authorities would learn. Little did I know that in hostels, it's the girls who need to learn! I signed on the form in reluctance, and bade good-bye to my local guardians who, like me, were clueless as to what lay ahead of me.

My room had six beds (for six people, of course!) and mine was the lousiest since I was the last one to join. Just as I was trying to push myself in through the aisle between the two beds, the warden came and said in the kind tone I was never to hear again during my stay, 'Don't worry, dear, you will soon be shifted to a two-seater.' All excited at my plunge into the big bad world, daddy's darling did not mind anything ... or at least she thought she didn't.

Evening set in and brought with it one of my room-mates. 'Hi, come down for dinner or it might get over soon.'

Lesson one: Mom is not around to feed you when you are late, leave alone the extra serving of your favorite sweet. Ever wondered why hostels call their dining rooms a 'mess'? Well I hadn't either but one look and I knew why. Picture this — more than two hundred girls cramped in a single room (no dearth of space, but girls will be girls), groups of eight trying to fit on a table for four and trying even harder to show that with their slim figures, they easily can.

Anyway, I did not have a choice but to follow the good samaritan who had woken me up. I sat on a chair waiting for my plate to be brought when the same 'you-better-learn girl' (I hated her) came to me and said in her best sarcastic tone, 'C'mon, you don't want to be served. Do you?'

Did I? I shook my head and said, 'Naah, just sitting for a while and waiting for things to settle down. You carry on, I'll join you later,' I said and looked around.

After a decent ten minutes of 'settling down', I got up and joined the queue for food. Another five minutes and I got a plate with some curry and rice. The curry smelt good, but what was it? I didn't want to look stupid on the first day, but had to know what I was eating. Wondering whom to ask, I overheard someone shouting, 'Marie, are you sure we won't find cockroaches in our chicken curry today?'

Amid giggles and laughter, my heart sank. I did not know what was worse — eating cockroaches or chicken? I was a pure vegetarian after all. 'Excuse me, can I have a veg plate please? I am a vegetarian actually,' I said to one of the kitchen girls. What followed next changed my whole life. She quietly picked up the chicken piece and replaced it with boiled potatoes with a smile. Her smile and that chicken-turned-potato curry changed my whole life. From a 'eat green, love-green' vegetarian, I transformed into a 'bone sucking, meat-chewing' non-vegetarian.

I wanted to call up my parents and cry my empty stomach out. But it was 9 p.m. already and I had no chance of going out to make any calls. I remembered the hostel phone but as I went to the 'pho roo' (phone-room) it seemed to be the day of family calling. Almost the entire hostel was there calling up their parents, brothers, boyfriends …. Lesson two: Dad is not your know-all super hero anymore. He obviously did not know about hostels when he promised me that he was just a call away.

I was lonely and sad and hungry and sleepy. So as the lights went off at 10 p.m., I cried myself to sleep, looking for respite in my dreams of a good, independent, 'vegetarian' life.

I don't know how long I was asleep but once again, I was shaken awake by someone. As I opened my eyes, it was not one but five smiling faces greeting me 'good morning'. I must have tried very hard to smile because one of them said, 'C'mon, hostel life is not all that difficult. We all learn despite the rules and the lousy food. Come, we've brought breakfast from outside, let's party.'

Suddenly, the same 'nice' Sister barged in screaming: 'You got food from outside!' My mom always says I am a good liar but I didn't realise how good I was till that moment. Something came over me that moment, because suddenly I jumped out of my bed and said, 'Oh! Sister, this is home-made. My mother got it for me yesterday. Would you like to have some too?'

Sister did not say a word or maybe she did. I don't know because the minute she was in the corridor, all I heard was my own laughter, gelling well with the 'gang'.

Lesson three: Home can't be everywhere, but you can be at home anywhere and friends, they can be everywhere.

Swaty Prakash

It's Just a Card

Shaina Thakkar was an intense girl in so many ways. She was passionate and ambitious, and although she never revealed it, she had a lot of empathy for her friends. While I felt privileged to be a part of the group of her friends, I thought of her more as a sister. We studied together for four years in high school before I changed schools. She was and will always be my best friend, and for others she will be something of a supporting soul. When we were fifteen, we studied for our Board exams — we went to tuition together and this strengthened our bond.

Aayana studied in our school and attended tuition classes with us. She was ordinary in many ways, overweight and with lanky brown hair. She wasn't beautiful, but was always smiling. Although I did not know her well, I had heard from others that she was a somewhat irritating person. How wrong I was!

It was the 23rd of December, an ordinary day for all of us. We had our math tuitions in the afternoon. All of us arrived, except Shaina. She came in a little late to class and sat down without a word. When class got over, we were all hanging around outside in the porch. Shaina suddenly hugged

Aayana and gave her a card. We were all embarrassed since none of us even knew that it was her birthday. Aayana burst into tears and confessed that she had never received a card in her life. It was an emotional moment. We all took turns to hug Aayana and apologised for not wishing her sooner.

She spoke to me and Shaina after every one left. She said that she had never had any real friends and was always lonely. People often believed all kinds of rumours that they heard about her and that definitely did not help matters. I felt guilty, knowing that I too had once believed the rumours. Shaina just consoled her and said, 'It's just a card after all! This is the least that I can do for a friend.' Aayana's eyes lit up at the word 'friend' and she smiled weakly once more.

After that, she became a friend and although she did not belong to our group, she was someone I made it a point to talk to, at least once or twice every day. She started talking about her problems to me and Shaina, instead of keeping them to herself. Gradually, as months passed, she became a much happier girl. One cannot say she was joyful, but at least when she was with us, she did not have a sad little smile anymore.

This episode with Aayana always makes me remember that words convey emotions much more effectively than anything else. And a letter is simply not a letter, a story is not a story, and a poem is not just a poem in a card that has been filled with love and care. So it's not, it's never, 'just a card'.

Shalvi Shah

Sing to My Heart

Said a wise man
'The heart is meant to be broken,'
But he never said
Of it being beaten and shaken.

In a mere twenty-four hours
And three-sixty-five days
The life you belonged to
Has become a misty haze.

White lies and red roses
Little stars in the velvet sky
Birthday wishes and happy memories
Love is something money can't buy.

Pop songs, love songs
Christmas lights, moonlight
Chic flicks, chocolate
Anything to get you through the night.
Curly hair and dark brown eyes
Words that turned the world around

In his eyes, a thousand galaxies,
Within his heart, forgiveness you found.

But now the music's too loud,
And the sun too bright,
The smile is untrue,
And the hugs are too tight.

Love is in dearth,
And resent and sorrow in over-drive,
Turn off the lights and run away,
Look for a dark place to hide.

Your mind is quiescent
Your thoughts worth more than a penny,
Now you've realised
This is your bitter epiphany.

Yet somewhere in this great universe
There exists a soul you are yet to meet
Courteous, brave, sincere and sharp
Someone certain to sweep you off your feet.

Meghna Anil

More Chicken Soup?

Share your heart with the rest of the world. If you have a story, poem or article (your own or someone else's) that you feel belongs in a future volume of Chicken Soup for the Indian Soul, please email us at cs.indiansoul@westland-tata. com or send it to:

Westland Ltd
S-35A, 3rd Floor
Green Park Main Market
New Delhi 110 016

We will make sure that you and the author are credited for the contribution. Thank you!

Contributors

Abhilasha Agarwal, a resident of Kolkata, works with a society called 'Kritagya' that looks after the aged. Her writings have been published in *The Statesman* and *The Times of India*. She is the author of the e-book *Vibrant Palette*. Her poetry has been exhibited by 'Jagori - 'Transportraits' at the India Habitat Centre. You can write to her at abcal37@yahoo.co.in.

Aditi Parikh is doing her B.Com from Ahmedabad. She likes creative writing and poetry and is an avid reader. She likes to engage in various intellectual and cultural activities like debates and theatre.

Advay Pal is thirteen, and studies at The Heritage School, Kolkata. He is an avid reader, keen sportsman and an aspiring fiction writer.

Agniv Basu is studying in class eight at The Heritage School. Passionate about football he gives his heart out to cheering his favourite team 'Real Madrid' and his favourite player, Kaka. His other interests are reading, music, hanging out with friends and playing all kinds of games. Agniv is fond of animals too. He can be reached at agniv_basu@yahoo.com.

Akanksha Singh is thirteen, and a class eight student of Anand Niketan, Ahmedabad. She is national level basketball player. She loves travelling, debating and hanging out with friends. She can be contacted at akki9711@gmail.com.

Akshika Agarwal can be reached at cool_girl_akshika@yahoo.co.in.

Anhad Mishra is in class seventh, studying in Bhopal. He has travelled widely, both within and outside India. Currently he is working on a book about his experiences during his latest expedition to East Timor.

Anupama Subramaniyam is a teenager, with a passion for writing and trying to pursue a career in it. Her other interests are music, reading, cooking and graphics. She can be reached at subra.anu@gmail.com.

Anushka Agarwal is studying interior design in Ahmedabad. She likes playing the guitar and listening to music. She can be reached at devilangels98@hotmail.com.

Archana Mohan is a business journalist based in Bangalore. She is a sports fanatic and a murder mystery addict. She blames global warming for her disastrous culinary skills and thanks god for instant noodles. She blogs at archanamohan.wordpress.com.

Arjun K. Bose is a businessman by profession, He has always been interested in literature, the fine arts and music. In fact, creative writing has been his secret hobby, which he has zealously guarded. He spent his initial years growing up in the hills in North Point, Darjeeling, till violence crept in and broke the serenity of the mountains. This story is not only a dedication to the innocence of the hills, but also to his alma mater, his wonderful boarding school, and all his dear friends. He can be contacted at basuarjun@gmail.com.

Arti Sonthalia is a budding writer, whose inspiration is her guru and to whose 'lotus feet' she attributes all her works. She resides in Hyderabad and writing is her passion. She can be contacted at 13artiag@gmail.com.

Ashima Suri is an entrepreneur, choreographer, writer and public speaker. She owns an Indo-contemporary dance theatre company called Limitless Productions (www.limitlessproductions.ca) where she uses performance art to convey real stories about South Asian life, culture and human emotions. She has also written for publications such as *Suhaag* magazine and *Fusia*. She can be reached at limitlessdance@gmail.com.

Ashita Chandran is presently pursuing her M Phil degree in English Literature from Madras Christian College, Chennai. An avid reader, her tastes vary from Dostoevsky to Asterix and Obelix. She hopes to take to writing full time someday. She can be reached at achandran09@gmail.com.

Avantika Debnath, or **Avni**, is a simple girl who believes that every pleasant story should be shared with the world around. However, some stories that do not have a pleasant end should be given a pleasant turn and left incomplete. She can be reached at avantika.debnath@gmail.com.

Ayushi Agarwal is a student of NIFT Ahmedabad, and is interested in pursuing fashion photography. Write to her at devilangels_28@yahoo.co.in.

Banani Saikia is a student doing her B.Com at Ahmedabad. She aspires to become a civil servant. Writing was never her hobby, and she is grateful to a few special friends and family who supported her in this endeavour. She loves playing tennis and sketching. Contact her at saikia.banani@gmail.com or 26767634.

Debashish Majumdar writes teen fiction. His stories are published in magazines like *Chandamama*, *Tinkle* and *Children's World*. His freelance works have appeared in *Deccan Herald*, *The Statesman*, *The Times of India*, *The Telegraph* (*Telekids*), *Indian Express* to name a few. He is a reputed speaker on parenting issues in schools. Contact him at debcreations@rediffmail.com.

Deepika wakes up everyday dreaming of owning a cafe in the mountains. Then she rushes to earn a living. She's passionate about life, words, music, cooking, Darjeeling tea and the Indian Railways. Right now, she is busy understanding the finer nuances of human emotions and life. She can be reached at mencuckoo@gmail.com.

Deepti Menon has been a writer for as long as she can remember, and loves the sheer thrill of seeing her name in print. In 2002, her light-hearted book, *Arms and the Woman*, on life as seen through the eyes of an army wife, was published by Rupa Publishers, Delhi. She continues to write for various magazines and publications, and loves every moment of it. She can be contacted at deepsmenon_7@yahoo.com.

Dikshita Maheshwar is a prolific reader (of fiction, of course), an occasional painter, a guitar enthusiast, a music and movie buff, a cat and dog lover … and has recently started dabbling in writing as well. An extrovert by nature, an introvert when she chooses, she is currently studying in class eleven and aspires to be many things. She can be reached at dikshita.406@gmail.com or evanscentstarlight_8@yahoo.com.

Drishti Chawla is studying in Toronto, Canada. She was born and brought up in Mumbai. She is enjoying every minute of her life and loves sharing stories for the world to know. She can be reached at drishtichawla@hotmail.com.

Eva Bell is a gynaecologist and also a freelance writer. Her articles, short stories and children's stories have been published in magazines, newspapers, on the net, and in several anthologies. She is a published author of three novels, two children's books, and three e-books. Her web site is www.evabell.net and she also blogs at http://muddyloafers. blogspot.com.

Gayathri Povannan is a network engineer and freelance writer. Her articles have been published in *The Gulf News*, *The Hindu*, *Chicken Soup for the Indian Soul* series, as well as in technical and HR management web sites. She lives in Dubai with her husband, and two sons, who along with her family in India take turns to be the muse behind her writings. Gayathri can be reached at gayatripon@gmail.com.

Ghazala S. Hossain likes to write from her heart. Her stories reflect real life. However she is mostly known for her creative fiction stories. Two of her short stories were published last year in an anthology called *Ripples*. She lives in Kolkata with her husband and two children. You can find her on Facebook at http://www.facebook.com/ghazalahossain or email her at msghazalahossain@gmail.com.

Hamsini Ravi works in the communications division of a developmental organisation. She loves and practices all forms of journalism. She is also interested in reading and watching sports. A feminist at heart, Hamsini has taken part in campaigns condemning violence against women. She can be reached at ravi.hamsini@gmail.com.

Harshita Bartwal is a voracious reader, and currently studying in the twelvth grade at Delhi Public School, RK Puram. She is the president of the Art Club and her many versatile interests include a boundless passion for art and music, an incurable craze for historical fiction, a continual love for weaving stories and conjuring random characters out of thin air. She can be reached at hbartwal.velocity@gmail.com.

Inika Sharma has stayed in a number of locations including Japan and Singapore. She is currently residing in Mumbai, and studying in

Cathedral and John Connon school. In her free time she enjoys listening to music, playing different sports, reading and writing.

By day, **Jamshed Velayuda Rajan** (also known as Jammy), is Director - Products, India, at Nimbuzz and by night he is a wannabe stand-up comedian. He blogs about his wife and life (and in recent times, his three-year-old daughter too!) at www.ouchmytoe.com. He can be reached at jammy@ouchmytoe.com and 09971996581.

Joie Bose Chatterjee has degrees in English literature from St. Xaviers' College, Kolkata, and Jawaharlal Nehru University, New Delhi. She has previously worked as a freelance journalist with *The Telegraph* and is a regular contributor to *The Statesman*. A social-worker, she was earlier involved in teaching English and Dramatics both formally and informally. She is currently working on her first collection of short stories and can be reached at joiebose@gmail.com.

Kamalesh Babu J. is an engineering student who aspires to be an entrepreneur. An ardent reader, with a strong passion for writing, he currently resides in Coimbatore, Tamil Nadu, and will be shifting to the US to pursue his higher education. He can be reached at themightykingkong@gmail.com.

Kavya Lakhani is a student of SNK School, Rajkot. She has been a consistent writer on various subjects such as the girl child, problems of the 'common man' and has also penned several poems. She can be reached at kavyalakhani@rediffmail.com.

Khursheed Dinshaw is a Pune-based freelance writer with more than six hundred and twenty published articles in major Indian newspapers and magazines. An avid traveller, she writes on lifestyle, travel, health, food, trends, people and culture. She also undertakes editing for publications and can be reached at khursheeddinshaw@hotmail.com.

Lhouvina Angami is from Nagaland, and currently pursuing her undergraduation in Philosophy from Madras Christian College, Chennai. She loves singing and playing the guitar. She belongs to a music band that has performed in various programmes and competitions in Chennai and elsewhere. She can be reached at avino_solo4christ@yahoo.com.

Madhuri Jagadeesh is a Bachelor in Arts and a Masters in English Literature, She works as a training and development consultant and is singer/song-writer with the world fusion band 'MoonArra.' She can be reached at moonarra@gmail.com.

Malavika Roy Singh is a homemaker by day and a writer by night. She quit her corporate job as a financial analyst to embark on her creative writing interest. What started as a hobby has become a full time interest now. Before Chicken Soup, she blogged and had a few articles e-published on sites like 4indianwomen.com. *Chicken Soup for the Indian Teen Soul* is her launch pad in print. She can be reached at malavika_ismd@yahoo.co.in.

Malavika Thiagaraja writes poetry and short stories as a hobby. Her works are available on her blog at www.tmalavika.blogspot.com. She can be reached at tmalavika@gmail.com.

Manushi Desai is a teenager studying in Zydus School for Excellence. She is a passionate reader and believes that writing is a medium of expression that easily leads to an understanding of one's emotions. She can be reached at d_manushi@yahoo.in.

Meena Murugappan is a sixteen-year-old pharmacy student from Fairleigh Dickinson University, New Jersey. She was born in India, raised in Zambia, and now lives in the United States. She is an accomplished Bharatnatyam dancer, a passionate writer and an avid reader. Later in life, she hopes to work for an NGO and serve the vulnerable in least developed countries.

Meghna Anil is an unabashed daydreamer and eternal hobbyist. Her story-writing journey began at the age of eight, and she wrote beginnings for several stories, but never quite finished them. She enjoys her grandmother's cooking more than anything, and hopes to travel the world someday. She can be reached at meghna.anil@gmail.com.

Monika Pant is an English teacher with fifteen years experience at various levels. She is now reinventing herself as a writer and editor. She has authored several series of English course books. Her articles, poems and short stories have been published in various collections and she is currently writing a couple of novels. She can be reached at mpant65@gmail.com.

Mudra Rawal enjoys writing in her free time and her collection keeps on expanding as she staunchly believes that everything and everyone around her needs to be written about. You can drop her a line at mudra.rawal@gmail.com.

N. Chokkan, short for Naga Subramanian Chokkanathan, is a software consultant by profession, and trainer/author by interest. He works as a Director for CRMIT Solutions Limited, Bangalore, leading the Training and Innovation division. He writes in Tamil, his mother tongue, and English, and has authored many books in varied topics such as biographies, corporate histories, science and technology, self help, etc. He blogs regularly at http://nagachokkanathan.wordpress.com and can be reached at nchokkan@gmail.com.

Neelam Chandra works as a Director in RDSO, Lucknow, in the Indian Railways. Many of her stories and two of her books have been published. She has won the second prize in a competition organised by Pratham Books. One of her stories has won an award in a contest organised by the Children's Book Trust in 2009. She has also been awarded the second prize by Gulzar in a poetry contest organised by the American Society. She can be reached at neelamsaxena27@yahoo.com or 0522 2450251.

Nidhi Pathak is an MBA in marketing and currently works for an NGO. She has worked on a variety of projects that involved report writing, web writing and blogging. Nidhi loves writing fiction, real life stories and poetry. She has done a course on 'Writing Lives' from Oxford University, Department for Continuing Education. Nidhi aspires to bring out her collection of short stories and poetry. Read her work on her blog http://www.knottydcharisma.blogspot.com. She can be reached at nidhinautiyal07@rediffmail.com.

Nisha Nair can be reached at nairnisha2306@gmail.com.

Niyantri Ravindran can be reached at niyantri15@gmail.com.

Parth Patel is a class nine student of Adani Vidya Mandir, Ahmedabad. He aspires to be an engineer and continue writing as a hobby. He can be reached at patel.parthcool.parth@gmail.com.

Priya Narayan is currently studying Arts in the eleventh grade in DPS, Ahmedabad. She has a quirky sense of humour and enjoys reading books, writing short stories, songs and poems, watching movies and playing her guitar. She can be reached at fanclubpria@yahoo.com.

Priyanka Kadam has written short stories, essays and poems that have appeared in magazines, anthologies and on the Internet. She believes that love, if not expressed appropriately, can lose its significance as we mature into relationships. Having found and then lost, she is still a die-hard romantic. She can be reached at priyanka.kadam99@gmail.com.

Raamesh Gowri Raghavan is a poet and writer by night, and a copywriter by day. He lives in Thane near Mumbai and is considered funny company by his friends (at times!). He can be reached at azhvan@yahoo.co.in at the correspondent's risk.

Radhika Meganathan is an editor, scriptwriter, reviewer, writing coach, avid traveller, movie fanatic, guilty glutton and last but never the least, a loving daughter. She is the 2004 Indian recipient of Highlights USA Fellowship for children's writers and has published twelve picture books (with twenty more under production). She is based in Chennai and offers online and live writing workshops for budding writers. Write to her at contact@radhikameganathan.in.

Rajeev Goenka is a student of class twelve in La Martiniere for Boys, Kolkata. He likes to write poetry, play sports like hockey, squash and boxing. Contact: 9830478973.

Ram Kumar Swamy is a mechanical engineer-turned-journalist working with a leading publishing company. He has serious interest in film-making, trekking, walking, cycling, and having coffee while indulging in long chats with friends. Contact him at ram.chocolate@yahoo.com.

Ranjani Rengarajan Deoras works in the media and is an avid reader. She is hoping to write a good book one day and is waiting for inspiration to hit! She can be reached at ranju17@gmail.com.

Rashi Agarwal, a student, loves classical dance and is a lively, out-going person. She can be reached at rockin.rashi@gmail.com.

Ratnadip Acharya is an electrical engineer residing in Mumbai. Apart from writing, which is his first love, he often performs street magic shows. He loves travelling and he can be reached at rracharya@rcfltd.com, ratnadip76@gmail.com or 09819237962.

Reeti Roy is originally from Kolkata. Her work has been published in newspapers and magazines such as *The Statesman*, *The Telegraph*, *The Times of India* and *Femina*. Her travel writing has been published by Matador Network. She is currently pursuing a Masters degree in Social Anthropology at the London School of Economics and Political Science.

Reshmi A.R. is a freelance journalist who has worked in renowned Indian publications and TV channels. She can be reached on reshmi. ar@gmail.com.

Sadhika Pant is a student of class ten, studying in St. Agnes Loreto Day School, Lucknow. She is the editor of her school magazine. She likes sketching and painting and plans to pursue an art course from one of the leading art institutes. She has won prizes in inter-school events in creative writing and art contests. She can be reached at rippedoldjeans@ gmail.com.

Sanaea Patel is an avid travel writer who loves travelling, listening to music and reading non-fiction. She can be contacted at sanaea.patel@ hotmail.com.

Shalvi Shah is a student of AIS school in Ahmedabad. She loves reading, writing, music and is currently learning how to play the guitar. She loves to channel help, support and care through her poems and short stories, and is completely reinventing ideas on what the future holds for her. She can be reached at shalvishah7@gmail.com.

Shaphali Jain has lived in India, Hong Kong, Canada and now calls Tampa, Florida, her home, where she lives with her husband, two children and a dog, as well as numerous reptiles that reside, much to her deep anguish, in her backyard. She is a writer in every spare moment and after having put together a South Asian print publication called *City Masala* in Florida, she has started to devote more time to writing. She can be contacted at shaphalijain@gmail.com.

Shashi Agarwal is a homemaker and mother of two. She likes reading and writing. She can be reached at agarwalsash@gmail.com.

Shifa Maitra loves tales. Writing is something she has to do, though not for a living; it's what she does for life. She has written TV shows, live events, title tracks for TV shows, and songs for a feature film. She is a creative director at UTV Bindass and can be contacted at shifamaitra@ gmail.com.

Shivani Singh is a tenth grade student at St. Mary's School, Pune. She is an avid reader who writes book reviews for blogs and has posted multiple stories on the web. Besides writing, she is passionate about football and music, having learnt to play four instruments. She has a deep interest in gadgets and gizmos, and hopes to pursue a career in computers.

Shreya Kalra is a fourth year student in School of Law, Christ University, Bangalore. An ardent writer ever since school, she is a national level debater, both at school and now at college level, and also adjudicates debates. She has also been doing theatre at college level for four years now with a lot of accolades. She has recently started her blog http:// fortheloveoffashionandotherthings.blogspot.com. and can be reached at shreyakalra1@gmail.com.

Sigma Samhita is a tenth grade student. She loves to see new places. Music, dance, writing and reading happen to be her greatest passions. She can be reached at write2sigma@gmail.com or 0674-2354023.

Sneha Tulsian is a student of class tenth at La Martiniere for Girls, Kolkata. She likes reading, writing and debates. Contact her at sneha.tulsian@gmail.com.

Reading has been **Soma Karnavat's** passion even before she could actually read (Grandpa and Mom used to read stories to her). This twenty-two-year-old also loves crafts, travelling and cooking. She strongly believes that for making the world a better place to live, everyone must contribute their bit. She can be reached at somakarnavat@ rediffmail.com.

For **Soumyarka Gupta**, writing has always been an infatuation. A way to be heard and understood. Her belief in the power of words is unshakeable because the right word in the right context can make an immense difference. This romance with writing that began about a decade ago has now turned into a full-blown affair, contributing to her daily bread. Contact shom.gupta@gmail.com or +91 9999476466.

Stutee Nag is pursuing her BA, LL.B (Hons.) from PU, Chandigarh.

Suchithra Pillai is a journalist, currently working as senior reporter cum editor with *Career Direct*, an Edex Group publication. Her interests include writing poems, stories, drawing and dancing. She can be reached at suchithrapillai@gmail.com.

Swati Rajgharia is a writer and editor. She can be reached at 17/905 Heritage City, MG Road, Gurgaon or swatirajgarhia@yahoo.com.

Swaty Prakash is a former journalist with over ten years experience in print and electronic media. Now a full-time mom and freelance editor, she is often bitten by the writing bug and gets her inspiration from life and its spirit. She can be contacted at swatyprakash@gmail.com.

Tammana Pant loves writing stories, and would love feedback on the one published in this series. He can be reached at sanjupant30@yahoo. com.

T.S. Karthik is an MBA from the Indian Institute of Planning and Management, Chennai. He is a voracious reader and an aspiring writer. He has won several prizes in business quizzes. His he loves watching movies, plays and listening to music. He believes in inspiring and motivating people to achieve their dreams. Contact him at tskarthik13@ yahoo.com.

Vedika Chitnis is currently studying in the eleventh grade. She has a strong passion for reading, writing and public speaking. She thinks writing is the purest form of expression and invests time in it to express herself in the best possible way. She aspires to be an entrepreneur and would also like to write for a magazine or newspaper. She currently lives in Ahmedabad, Gujarat. Contact her at vedikachitnis@gmail.com.

Veerendra Mishra is a police officer from Madhya Pradesh. He is fond of writing fiction, books related to his profession, short stories, articles on social issues and the like.

Zainab Sulaiman is a freelance writer and businesswoman — she makes children's quilts under the Fatcat label, and is a busy mother of two young children. She writes a blog on the simple joys, challenges and rewards of parenting at www.memoriesofchocolate.wordpress.com and can be reached by email at fatcatbangalore@yahoo.com.

Permissions